DISCRIMINATION

AFRICAN AMERICANS STRUGGLE FOR EQUALITY

DISCRIMINATION

AFRICAN AMERICANS STRUGGLE FOR EQUALITY

by
ANNA WILSON

Rourke Corporation, Inc.
Vero Beach, Florida 32964

Cover design: David Hundley

∞ The paper used in this book conforms to the American
National Standard for Permanence of Paper for Printed
Library Materials, Z39.48-1984.

Library of Congress Cataloging-in-Publication Data
Wilson, Anna, 1970-
    African Americans struggle for equality / by Anna
Wilson.
        p.   cm. — (Discrimination)
    Includes bibliographical references and index.
    Summary: Identifies discrimination and discusses the
struggle of African Americans for equality in education,
employment, and other areas of life.
    ISBN 0-86593-184-4 (alk. paper)
    1. Race discrimination — United States — Juvenile liter-
ature.   2. Afro-Americans — Civil rights — Juvenile literature.   3. United States — Race relations — Juvenile
literature.   [1. Race discrimination.   2. Discrimination.   3. Afro-Americans — Civil rights.   4. Race relations.]   I. Title.   II. Series.
E185.625.W524   1992   92-16282
305.896'073 — dc20   CIP
                                                AC

PRINTED IN THE UNITED STATES OF AMERICA

CONTENTS

DISCRIMINATION

AFRICAN AMERICANS STRUGGLE FOR EQUALITY

1 What Is Discrimination?

A nation of immigrants, the United States enjoys the benefits of a truly multicultural society. In Los Angeles, California, Americans of every ethnic origin help ring in the Chinese New Year in Chinatown, celebrate Cinco de Mayo on Olvera Street, and choose from Moroccan, Italian, African, and even Russian cuisine. Every major city in the United States offers a similarly rich mix of cultures, as do many of the smaller towns. Unfortunately, the land of opportunity, prosperity, and freedom has been troubled since its birth by conflict between the many groups that make up its citizenry. Discrimination is a problem that has persistently plagued the American people. The number of newspaper headlines devoted to the topic make it obvious that discrimination is very much a problem in the 1990's. "U.S. Accuses a TV Station of Sex Discrimination" (*New York Times*, November 21, 1990), "Pillsbury to Pay $3.6 Million to Settle Discrimination Suit" (*Washington Post*, October 13, 1990), "Atlanta Symphony Accused of Age Discrimination" (*Atlanta Constitution*, April 13, 1990). The headlines also show how widespread the problem is; the "President Calls for End to AIDS Discrimination" (*Washington Post*, March 30, 1990), and the *Chicago Tribune* questions, "Are the Boy Scouts Guilty of Religious Discrimination?" (June 13, 1991). No American is unaffected by the presence of discrimination.

The term "discrimination" is used in connection with such vastly different situations and is so closely tied to prejudice (including racism, sexism, ageism, etc.) that the meaning of the word can be easily confused. Discrimination, the act of choosing between alternatives, can be an acceptable process of selection. For example, without exception, professional jockeys are very small individuals. Discrimination against larger riders is based on the fact that a horse carrying more weight cannot run as fast. The decision is based on a characteristic which would actually affect the outcome of a race so it is a valid, productive decision. In contrast, the forms of discrimination that are forbidden by law lack a legitimate basis. For example, when an employer consistently hires male applicants instead of equally qualified female applicants, the employer is practicing unjust discrimination. Unjust discrimination is the topic of the series to which this book belongs.

The Roots of Prejudice

The difference between prejudice and discrimination is the difference between attitude and action. A prejudice is a negative *feeling* about people based on their membership in a specific population group but discrimination always refers to *action* against members of a group. It is natural to assume that prejudice lies behind discrimination, that feeling leads to action, and in many cases it does. Thus, in an attempt to fully understand discrimination, it is important to consider what lies behind prejudice.

Many people "learn" their prejudices at home from their families and friends, and at school from peers, teachers, and even textbooks. This process, termed cultural transmission, occurs when members of a younger generation accept the shared beliefs that exist in their home and community. Often, these beliefs include stereotypes, the false belief that individuals who belong to a group necessarily share certain characteristics with the other members of the group. Stereotypes are so easily and subtly transmitted that they are one of the most common manifestations

In countless ways, victims of prejudice and discrimination are made to feel that they are inferior. (Library of Congress)

of prejudice. Of course, not everyone accepts the prejudices of their home community; there is often disagreement even between family members. Two sons in one family could grow up only one or two years apart, in contact with the same neighbors, the same teachers, and the same kids at school, and develop totally different views of society. Instances such as this make it clear that prejudice is not just a result of cultural transmission.

One factor that could account for the differing opinions of people who were raised under identical circumstances is a difference between their personalities. Some sociologists suggest that although accepting group stereotypes is normal behavior, the person who allows those stereotypes to develop into prejudice does so because of an unconscious "need." The theory is that negative feelings of guilt, fear, and insecurity can create the need to look down on other people. When influenced by stereotypes present in the community, this need takes the form of prejudice against an entire group.

The way people deal with the frustrations of everyday life is another instance in which there is a connection between personality and prejudice. Some people deal with life's inevitable disappointments more easily than others. When a person is unable to cope, frustration often leads to anger for which there is no reasonable outlet. This anger is often "taken out" on an innocent target. When irrational anger is repeatedly directed toward an entire group, the aggressor will readily accept unfavorable stereotypes to justify his actions. Thus, unless a person with this tendency learns to vent his frustration in another way, the stereotypes will become ingrained as prejudice. Although minority groups are often targets, individual members of minority groups follow the same pattern of frustration and aggression leading toward prejudicial hatred of the majority group.

It is important to realize that prejudice is not just a matter of an individual's experience or personality. As a member of a dominant group, a person can enjoy economic advantages: higher pay, upper-level positions, and consequently, nicer housing, better schools and other real benefits. However, workers who receive inflated wages only because they are members of the dominant group cannot feel secure in their position because the availability of cheaper labor in the subordinate group or groups represents a constant threat. Dominant-group workers defend their privileges by claiming to be superior to the subordinate groups; they base their claims on unfavorable stereotypes. In combination with the intense feelings of hostility that result from continual competition, the stereotypes become intrenched as prejudice in many individuals who benefit from the dominance of the entire group to which they belong.

The idea of belonging to a group can, in itself, lead to prejudice. People tend to look at the world in terms of "we" and "they," or "we" against "they." When speaking of ethnic groups, sociologists call this attitude ethnocentrism. Beginning with a person's belief that his own group is "normal" and does things the "right" way, ethnocentrism usually leads to rejection of other groups and their differing practices. This tendency occurs naturally wherever people are divided into more than one group, but it is a problem when as many groups as make up the American citizenry live in such close quarters.

There is no single cause of prejudice. Many factors work together in the development of such a deeply rooted, destructive attitude. To reduce discrimination caused by prejudice, we must consider all the various circumstances that generate prejudice. People disagree about which factors are the most important, and this makes it hard to decide which strategy would be most effective in combating prejudice. The problem of discrimination is complicated further by the fact that it is not always a result of prejudice. Sometimes, discrimination is caused directly by factors other than prejudice. In these cases, discrimination can instead lead to prejudice so that there is a circular relationship between the two.

Discriminatory Behavior

As with prejudice, discriminatory behavior often begins early in childhood. Cultural transmission contributes to prejudice as biases and stereotypes pass through a community from one generation to the next. Discrimination results when modes of behavior are passed on in the same way. Children learn through imitation, so it is important that they mimic the behavior of older individuals in their community. Unfortunately, they will pick up the bad with the good. Children can discriminate without knowing what they are doing. Their actions are not based on the same feelings as the person they are mimicking. Eventually, though, many children "learn" the feelings of prejudice that logically accompany discriminatory behavior. In this way, the circle is established, so that the prejudice and the discrimination feed into and sustain each other.

Although the advantages of belonging to a dominant group can motivate individuals to harbor prejudices that "justify"

Many black people feel that they are under pressure from coworkers and supervisors to "act white," to conform to white expectations. (Library of Congress)

discriminatory behavior, prejudice is not always a part of the relationship between discrimination and "group gains." When it is profitable to discriminate, people will discriminate even if they aren't prejudiced. This means that even if the problem of prejudice is reduced, discrimination may continue. For example, if one group of people gets higher paying jobs than another because of discrimination, the group that benefits may continue to discriminate.

Social pressures also encourage discriminatory behavior. A man who objects to discrimination in theory may be a member of the racially exclusive social club to which his friends belong. Parents who consider themselves completely unprejudiced might oppose the interracial marriage of one of their children. At the same time, many people who confess to being prejudiced do not actively discriminate. A person who frequently stereotypes other groups might maintain mutually beneficial relationships with members of the groups against whom he or she is biased. Whether the relationship is between business associates or neighbors, something in the situation keeps the prejudiced individual from acting on his instincts. Since social pressures can determine whether or not discrimination takes place regardless of the prejudice of individuals, efforts to reduce discrimination must work on entire social standards.

Institutional Discrimination

The most difficult form of discrimination to eliminate goes beyond individual prejudice, beyond individuals altogether. It is anchored in the various systems that function together to create American society. Although American institutions, such as schools, hospitals, and banks, have employment requirements that would seem fair because they are uniform, the requirements automatically rule out people whose experience differs from the desired norm. If a woman who has spent many years working as a homemaker decides to look for work outside the home, she will probably have trouble finding a good job. Many jobs require experience, and the woman's time away from the work force would make her ineligible even if she had a college degree. Similarly, a person who has suffered through discrimination in the school system and who therefore does not have a high school or college diploma will not have the same employment opportunities as more privileged members of society. Growing up in a household in which a parent has been subject to discrimination can affect the choices a person makes, especially about jobs and education. Often, the person will make choices that lead to exclusion from otherwise equal opportunities. Many teenagers who grow up in relative poverty drop out of high school in favor of low paying jobs because they so badly want to

Institutional discrimination makes it easy for people to accept and perpetuate injustice; "that's just the way things are." (Library of Congress)

make money. In this way, they exclude themselves from higher paying jobs that require a high school or college diploma. The result of a chain such as this is referred to as institutional discrimination.

Discrimination Hurts Everyone

Who is affected by discrimination and related issues? Who will benefit from the elimination of discrimination? Who is discriminated against? The answers to these questions emphasize the importance of dealing with the problem of discrimination. Current law prohibits employers from discriminating on the basis of race, color, religion, national origin, sex, age, marital status, personal appearance, sexual orientation, family responsibilities, physical handicap, matriculation, and political affiliation. According to this law, everyone has attributes on which discrimination can be based. You may not be a member of an ethnic minority but you are male or female and may be subject to discrimination based on that fact alone. Every person is a potential victim of discrimination; thus, every person must be protected.

It can be argued that people who discriminate suffer as a result of their own actions. When we treat other people unfairly, we diminish ourselves, too. And if we don't join the fight against discrimination, there is always the chance that we will find ourselves victimized by it at some point in our lives. Whether we discriminate or are discriminated against, everyone suffers as a part of a society that allows such a destructive process to continue.

2 The African American Experience

The history of any group of people is actually made up of countless individual life-stories, only a few of which are ever recorded for others to read about and learn from. When we talk about the African American experience, we need to remember that it is not one story but many, woven into a pattern of suffering and beauty and infinite complexity; no one book — not even a hundred books — can tell the "whole story" of black Americans and their struggle for equality.

The story of black Americans begins with slavery. Most people who live in the United States today are the descendants of immigrants who came to this country by choice. Many of these immigrants came in search of equality. They wanted a fair chance to own land, to have a good job. They wanted to be able to practice their religion freely. They wanted to participate in a political system that honored the rights of the individual.

In contrast, most black Americans today are the descendants of slaves, brought to the United States from Africa against their own will. Instead of equality, they found the most brutal form of discrimination. The slaves were regarded as property. Though some white people protested against slavery and eventually helped to abolish it, many whites treated the slaves as if they

A Slave-Coffle passing the Capitol.

The terrible reality of slavery made a mockery of America's claim of liberty and justice for all. (Library of Congress)

were less than human. Even among the whites who fought against slavery there were many who believed that black people were inferior to whites.

The attitudes that developed during that time did not disappear when slavery was legally abolished. In the 1960's, a hundred years after President Abraham Lincoln's Emancipation Proclamation, black Americans still suffered from blatant discrimination. But a change was coming. In the 1950's, key court decisions had affirmed the right of black people to equality in education and in other areas of public life. In the 1960's, the black struggle for equality became a nationwide movement.

The Civil Rights movement was led by many inspiring figures — above all, Dr. Martin Luther King, Jr. — but what made the movement effective was the determination of tens of thousands of ordinary people — black Americans who demanded their right to equal treatment under the law. The black Civil Rights movement aroused the nation's conscience, encouraging other victims of discrimination to organize and demonstrate for their rights.

The entire history of African Americans, from the arrival of the first black indentured servants in Jamestown, Virginia, in 1619, to the triumphs of the Civil Rights movement in the 1960's, has been a battle against discrimination. (For suggestions for further reading in African American history, see the Bibliography at the end of the book.) Our focus in this book, however, is on the present — on the struggle for equality that is still going on in the 1990's.

Toward an Integrated Society

The African American community today is a study in contradictions. On the one hand, there are many signs that the barriers of racial prejudice and discrimination have finally been broken down. Black Americans have never played such a prominent part in the nation's life as they do today.

Virtually all of the major cities of the United States — cities such as New York, Los Angeles, Chicago, Washington, D.C., Philadelphia, Detroit, and Atlanta — either are currently led by a black mayor or recently had a black mayor in office. Before the Civil Rights era, this would have been impossible. Cities such as Denver, Kansas City, and Seattle have also elected black mayors.

In 1947, the Brooklyn Dodgers made headlines with Jackie Robinson, the outstanding black player who broke baseball's "color line." Today, it is hard to believe that there was actually a time when professional sports were segregated. Almost all of the starting players in the National Basketball Association are black,

Duke Ellington and his band; the black contribution to American culture is immeasurable.
(Library of Congress)

and black players are also heavily represented in professional baseball and football.

The most popular television series of the 1980's was "The Cosby Show," a show about a black family, created by its star, the gifted comedian Bill Cosby. The popularity of "The Cosby Show" wasn't limited to black audiences, nor to audiences in the United States. Like Michael Jackson and other black entertainers, Bill Cosby reached audiences throughout the world.

Black voices have always influenced American culture, even during the long period of segregation, when they were officially excluded from public life. To take just one example, think of the 1920's, "the Jazz Age," a period which drew much of its inspiration from the vibrant black culture. Today, however, black voices are more widely heard than ever before, from the angry rap of Public Enemy to the films of Spike Lee and John Singleton, from the plays of August Wilson to the novels of Alice Walker and Toni Morrison.

Few events in recent memory have so completely absorbed the nation's attention as the liberation of Kuwait in 1991. The chairman of the Joint Chiefs of Staff of the U.S. armed forces, the architect of the stunning victory of the United States and its allies over Saddam Hussein's Iraq, was Colin Powell, a black man born in Harlem to Jamaican immigrants and reared in the Bronx.

All of these examples — and many others could be cited — show genuine progress toward a truly integrated society. This progress has not been limited to celebrities; it has changed the everyday life of black people. Colleges and universities that once excluded blacks now actively seek black students. Black people have a much wider choice of jobs than they did in the past, and the black middle class continues to grow. There have been dramatic changes in other areas as well. In the mid-1960's, for example, infant mortality claimed more than forty black babies per one thousand births (the white rate was 21.5 per one thousand births); by 1988, the black infant mortality rate had shrunk to 17.6 per one thousand births.

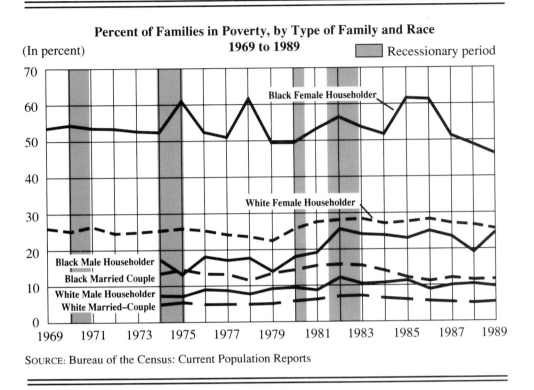

Percent of Families in Poverty, by Type of Family and Race
1969 to 1989

(In percent)   ☐ Recessionary period

SOURCE: Bureau of the Census: Current Population Reports

A Community at Risk

Many black Americans feel that positive stories about black
life are often ignored or underplayed by the media. At the same
time, there is a real sense of crisis in the black community today.
Despite the gains of the Civil Rights movement, millions of black
people still live in segregated neighborhoods, many in decaying
inner cities ravaged by drug abuse and by the violent crime
associated with the drug trade.

Despite massive busing programs and other efforts to integrate
public education, many black children still attend schools which
are more than 90 percent nonwhite. Typically these schools are
overcrowded and underequipped, desperately in need of
textbooks, supplies, and basic repairs.

Infant Mortality Rates by Race, 1940-1988

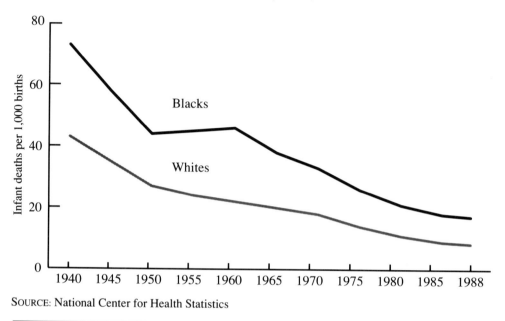

SOURCE: National Center for Health Statistics

In some ways, conditions in the black community are worse than they were before the Civil Rights era. In 1950, only 17 percent of black households were headed by single women. In 1990, 56 percent of black households were headed by single women. Many black children grow up without ever having the support of a father. In 1990, more than 60 percent of black births were out of wedlock.

Measuring Inequality

In the chapters that follow, we will look more closely at the ongoing struggle of black Americans for equality in education, labor and employment, and other areas of life. To judge the progress that has been made in that struggle, we'll sometimes cite statistics, as we have already in this chapter.

A Ku Klux Klan rally; even today, such groups continue to preach racial hatred. (Mark Reinstein/Uniphoto)

Statistics are invaluable for measuring realities that are too complex to be directly observable. Statistics are valuable in another way too. We all have our share of erroneous ideas, based on "common sense" and inherited prejudices. An encounter with a belligerent red-haired motorist may lead us to conclude that, yes, the folk-wisdom is correct, redheads *are* temperamental — forgetting as we do so all the calm redheads we've encountered but haven't noticed. Statistics provide us with a reality-check, challenging such dubious generalizations.

Yet for all their usefulness, statistics are very treacherous as well. If you want to make a particular point, you can usually find a statistic to support it. Earlier we mentioned the dramatic decrease in the black infant mortality rate between 1965 and 1988. That statistic provides evidence of progress toward racial equality. However, the black rate in 1988 (17.6 per one thousand births) was still more than twice as high as the white rate of infant mortality in 1988 (8.5 per one thousand births). That statistic suggests that equality has not yet been achieved. Taken alone, either statistic would be partial and misleading. Statistics always require interpretation. Use them with caution — including the ones in this book.

The Debate Over Causes

Why is the unemployment rate among black men so high? Why are standardized test scores for black students consistently lower than scores for students from other racial and ethnic groups? Why are blacks so disproportionately represented in the prison population? Questions such as these continue to provoke heated debate both inside and outside the black community, with a wide range of answers and no consensus.

Clearly, in part the answer lies in history. The long-term effects of slavery and segregation cannot be overcome in a generation. But what about right now, today? Legal barriers to inequality have been removed, but what about more subtle barriers?

Racial discrimination still exists in the United States, and black people still suffer from it. The extent to which racism is responsible for all of the ills that besiege African Americans is less certain. What is certain is that no one, black or white, can afford to be satisfied with simplistic answers that put the blame on everyone else. Only together shall we truly overcome.

Jamaican Americans who have succeeded financially return to the island to visit relatives; immigration from Jamaica increased beginning in the 1960's. (Justin K. Anderson)

3 Education

In 1991, a junior high school in Harlem, named after the black congressman Adam Clayton Powell, Jr., fielded a national championship team — in chess. Maurice Ashley, a young black chess professional, had begun working with the team, the Raging Rooks, in 1989. The Rooks did well in the 1990 national tournament, and in 1991 they tied for the championship.

The Rooks' victory opened some eyes. "For kids," Ashley said later, in an interview in *The New Yorker* magazine, "it's what they see. And they don't see black chess players, or blacks in intellectual fields at all. It's when the kids start *seeing* these paths that they become possibilities in their minds, and then it's not a shock to them that Harlem kids can be national chess champions."

Given the opportunity, black students can excel. Jaime Escalante received national acclaim for his advanced calculus courses at Garfield High School in East Los Angeles, where most of the students are Hispanic, as seen in the movie *Stand and Deliver*.

Not many people know, however, that in the 1970's Philip Uri Treisman, a professor at the University of California at Berkeley, achieved similar success with black students in early calculus courses there. The key is equality of opportunity — and that is something that has been denied to African American people for much of their history.

Separate and Unequal

In 1944, A. Leon Higginbotham, Jr. was one of twelve black freshmen entering Purdue University. Unlike the white students, who roomed in a comfortable, heated dormitory, the black students—all twelve of them—were assigned to an unheated attic.

It gets cold in Indiana. After a couple of freezing winter months, Higginbotham went to talk to the president of the university, Edward Charles Elliott, to ask him if room for the black students could be found in the dormitory. The president replied, "Higginbotham, the law doesn't require us to let colored students in the dorm and we will never do it." That exchange, Higginbotham says, prompted him to become a lawyer. He was graduated from Yale Law School and eventually became a federal appeals judge.

The circumstances in which Higginbotham and his fellow students found themselves were typical for black students at that time, starting in elementary school and going all the way through the educational system. Only at black institutions such as Howard University could black students count on being treated as equals.

The legal basis for the discrimination which Higginbotham encountered at Purdue was an 1896 Supreme Court decision, *Plessy v. Ferguson*. In that decision, the Court ruled that segregated public facilities were permissible, as long as the separate facilities for whites and blacks were equal.

In practice, of course—especially in the South, where segregation was more rigid than it was in the rest of the country—the "facilities" provided for black people were not equal to those for whites. But aside from the obvious inequities it perpetuated, the "separate but equal" doctrine had a more insidiously damaging effect on black people. Segregation constantly sent a message to black people that they were inferior to whites.

A school for black children, c. 1939, typical of conditions during the "separate but equal" era. (Library of Congress)

Desegregation and Black Gains in Education

The effect of the "separate but equal" doctrine was particularly evident in education, and it was there that the Supreme Court finally reversed itself, rejecting the principle that had been established with *Plessy v. Ferguson*. In a 1954 decision, *Brown v. Topeka Board of Education*, the Court ruled that segregated schools were inherently unequal, even if they were equally well-staffed and supplied.

Now in fact, as we have noted, public schools for black students were generally not equal to public schools for whites in terms of facilities. But even if they were equal in those terms, the Court ruled, they would not provide equal educational opportunities. Drawing in part on the pioneering work of the black psychologist Kenneth B. Clark, the Court emphasized that segregated schooling fostered a sense of inferiority in black students.

For a period of roughly thirty years following this decision, large-scale efforts were made to desegregate America's school systems and, at last, to provide black students with equal opportunities to excel. As a result of these efforts, which gained force as the Civil Rights movement grew, the black community has experienced substantial gains in education.

In 1960, only about 280,000 black Americans were college graduates; in 1992, the total is well over two million. In 1968, almost fifteen years after *Brown v. Topeka Board of Education*, the percentage of black children in public education attending intensely segregated schools (schools 90 percent or more black) was still quite high: 64 percent. By 1980, that percentage had been cut almost in half, to 33 percent. (Since that time, however, the percentage of black children attending intensely segregated schools has not changed significantly.)

Even in the 1980's, a decade which saw blacks lose ground in some areas, there were substantial gains as well. In 1980, for example, 62.2 percent of black males between thirty-five and

Students at Alabama A&M University; today, many historically black colleges are enjoying an increase in enrollment. (Ron Sherman/Uniphoto)

forty-four years old had completed four years of high school or more; by 1990, that figure had increased to 78.9 percent. Black females registered a slightly higher increase, from 62.8 percent in 1980 to 80.7 percent in 1990.

Such statistics don't indicate the full range of black gains in education. In part as a result of affirmative action (see chapter 7), colleges and universities have been making an ongoing effort to increase black enrollment. At the same time, they have actively recruited black faculty. In fact, the nation's most prestigious universities are competing with one another to add leading black scholars to their faculties.

Another important gain in educational opportunity for blacks began in the 1960's, when programs in Black Studies or African

American Studies were first established. These programs encouraged black students to value themselves and their cultural heritage. While traditional textbook history had largely ignored the contributions of black Americans, these programs highlighted black achievements in every area of endeavor.

The Persistence of Inequality

It is important to keep in mind the enormous black gains in education, which are too often forgotten in the debate over current problems. It is clear, though, that the battle is far from being won, for evidence of continuing inequality can be found at every hand.

For example, 70 percent of black students at four-year colleges drop out at some point during their college career; some return and complete their studies, but many do not. For white students, the figure is 49 percent. According to an NCAA study, black athletes at Division 1 colleges are only half as likely as white athletes to graduate.

Whether or not they are athletes, many black students enter college at a serious academic disadvantage. While average SAT scores for blacks have increased since the 1960's, over a period that has seen a slight decline in average SAT scores for whites, there is still a huge gulf between black and white scores: in 1990, average scores for blacks were 737; for whites, 933.

The most disturbing evidence of persisting inequality in education, however, is not to be found at the college level, nor can it be adequately measured by test scores or similar tools. This evidence is to be found in the inner-city elementary schools and secondary schools where a substantial number of black children are educated.

How substantial a number? Between 25 and 30 percent of black children in the public schools are enrolled in the twenty-five largest urban school districts in the United States. Almost without exception, these urban discricts are in areas that have experienced

Percent of High School Graduates 18 to 24 Years Old Enrolled in College, by Sex and Race: October 1970, 1980, and 1988

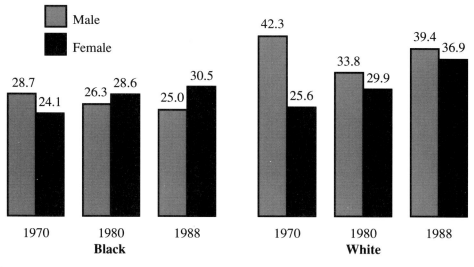

SOURCE: Bureau of the Census: Current Population Reports

Percent of Persons 35 to 44 Years Old Who Have Completed 4 Years of High School or More, by Sex and Race: 1980 and 1990

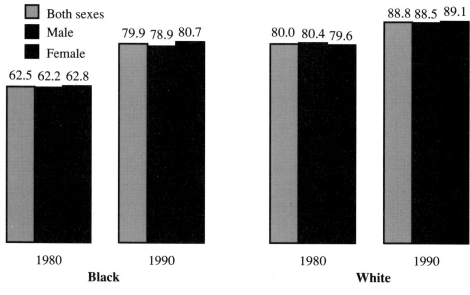

SOURCE: Bureau of the Census: Current Population Reports

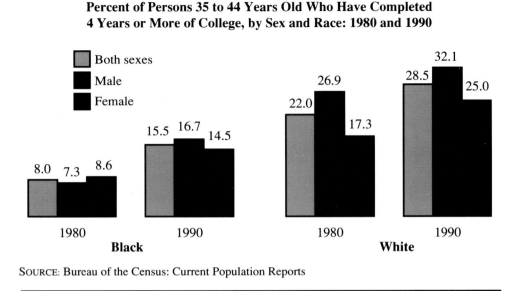

Percent of Persons 35 to 44 Years Old Who Have Completed 4 Years or More of College, by Sex and Race: 1980 and 1990

Both sexes
Male
Female

Black: 1980 — 8.0, 7.3, 8.6; 1990 — 15.5, 16.7, 14.5

White: 1980 — 22.0, 26.9, 17.3; 1990 — 28.5, 32.1, 25.0

SOURCE: Bureau of the Census: Current Population Reports

severe losses in business and industry and sharply declining property values. They are in areas beset by crime and drugs, and often by environmental pollution, areas where unemployment is much higher than the national average. Only about 3 percent of white children in the public schools are enrolled in these districts.

Between 1988 and 1990, Jonathan Kozol, a former teacher and a writer on issues relating to education, poverty, and homelessness, visited some of these districts, in places such as East St. Louis, Illinois; Chicago; New York City; Camden, New Jersey; Washington, D.C.; and San Antonio, Texas. He reported what he saw and heard there in a 1991 book, *Savage Inequalities: Children in America's Schools*.

Kozol visited schools and talked with principals, teachers, and, especially, the children themselves. Again and again he has the same story to tell. Almost forty years after *Brown v. Topeka Board of Education*, these schools are intensely segregated — most of them, Kozol says, 95 to 99 percent nonwhite. Class sizes are too large, and the facilities are hopelessly inadequate. These schools don't simply lack computers; they don't even have equipment for chemistry labs.

Often in close proximity to these decaying schools — just across the river or up the hill — there are superbly equipped suburban schools, with primarily white enrollments. Because funding for the schools depends largely on the relative affluence of the local districts, there is a great disparity in spending per pupil. In Camden, for example, spending per pupil is $3,538; in nearby suburban Cherry Hill, $5,981; in Princeton, $7,725.

As Kozol observes, it is the children from depressed urban districts who need the most help in school, to balance at least in part the disadvantages they start with. Instead, the disparity in school funding ensures that the gap between the fortunate and the less-fortunate will increase.

4 Employment

From the beginning, African Americans have worked at many different jobs. Even during the period of slavery, there were free blacks in the North practicing medicine and law, operating businesses, teaching school. They became the foundation of the black middle class, whose history is often ignored in overviews of the African American experience.

Nevertheless, for much of their history most black Americans have been limited by discrimination in their choice of employment. Moreover, they have also been vulnerable to discrimination in the workplace. As recently as 1968, the Kerner Commission report stated that "Negro workers are concentrated in the lowest-skilled and lowest-paying occupations. These jobs often involve substandard wages, great instability and uncertainty of tenure, extremely low status in the eyes of both the employer and employee, little or no chance for meaningful advancement, and unpleasant or exhausting duties."

For 1968, that assessment was too pessimistic, but it accurately describes the circumstances of many black workers from the period of Reconstruction to the 1950's, and it still applies to some black workers today. In 1950, for example, about 40 percent of black female employees worked in domestic service (cooking, cleaning, and performing similar duties within the homes of their employers). This hard, ill-paid work certainly fits the description from the Kerner Commission report. (By 1980, fewer than 5 percent of black female employees worked as domestics.)

Many blacks responded to discrimination by seeking employment within their own community. Black teachers,

A government charwoman, c. 1940; under segregation, the majority of black workers were restricted to low-paying, menial jobs. (Library of Congress)

ministers, undertakers, barbers — figures such as these played an important role in their community. Instead of being defined by the white world, their jobs were defined by the needs and preferences of their own people. (Before World War II, as Thomas Byrne Edsall and Mary D. Edsall note, an astonishing 73 percent of black college graduates became either teachers or ministers — a good indication of the limited choices available to blacks at that time.)

Because blacks were concentrated in lower-paying jobs, and because they were generally paid less than whites were for the same work, black women had to enter the labor force in large numbers before their white counterparts did. (Today, the percentages of black women and white women who work outside the home are virtually identical.)

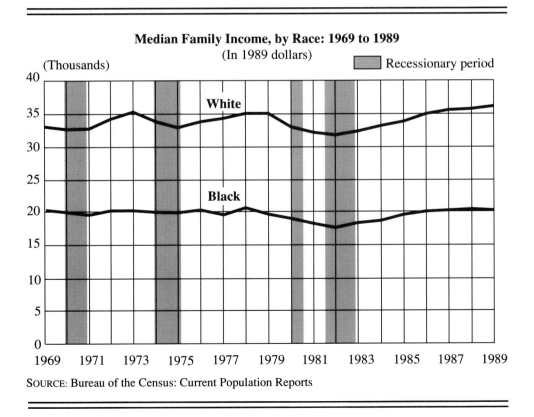

Median Family Income, by Race: 1969 to 1989
(In 1989 dollars)

SOURCE: Bureau of the Census: Current Population Reports

Black Gains in Employment

Many interrelated factors brought about significant gains in black employment beginning in the 1960's. The Civil Rights movement and the legislation it prompted (see chapter 7, "Affirmative Action"), the growth of the black middle class, changes in the American economy — these and other factors all contributed.

Some of these changes, in other words, resulted from a concerted effort to end discrimination against blacks, while others did not. In analyzing social change, it is often difficult to identify precisely what caused what. Why were these economic gains of blacks accompanied by the growth of a "culture of poverty" in the inner cities, a chronically poor, welfare-dependent "underclass"? Social scientists, policymakers, and others who have addressed this important question disagree strongly, proposing many different answers.

Attention to the problems of the inner cities has tended to obscure the real gains in black employment. Between 1950 and 1990, the black population doubled, but during that same period the number of blacks holding white-collar jobs increased by more than nine times. In the 1970's, the number of black women entering executive, administrative, or managerial jobs increased 14 percent annually; for black men, there was an 8 percent annual increase.

Black increases in executive, administrative, and managerial jobs are particularly important, since they suggest the breaking down of prejudice and discrimination. An increasing number of white employees work under black supervisors with no special tensions on either side.

Other black employment gains also indicate a decline in prejudice and discrimination. Between 1970 and 1990, while the black labor force as a whole increased by 60 percent, the number of black police officers increased by more than 250 percent; the number of black pharmacists more than tripled, as did the number of black electricians.

Blacks and Whites by Occupation, 1990

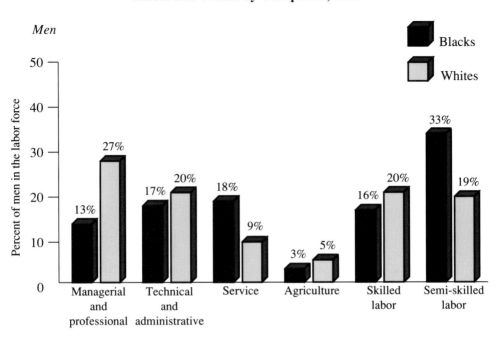

Men

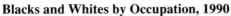

Blacks

Whites

Percent of men in the labor force

50 —
40 —
30 —
20 —
10 —
0 —

| Managerial and professional | Technical and administrative | Service | Agriculture | Skilled labor | Semi-skilled labor |

13% 27% 17% 20% 18% 9% 3% 5% 16% 20% 33% 19%

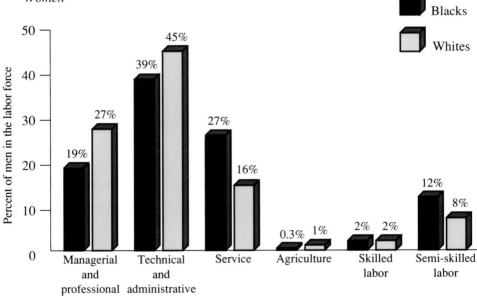

Women

Blacks

Whites

Percent of men in the labor force

50 —
40 —
30 —
20 —
10 —
0 —

| Managerial and professional | Technical and administrative | Service | Agriculture | Skilled labor | Semi-skilled labor |

19% 27% 39% 45% 27% 16% 0.3% 1% 2% 2% 12% 8%

SOURCE: Bureau of Labor Statistics

Shacks of black migrant workers in the 1940's. (Library of Congress)

Black Entrepreneurship

Recently, communities in both New York City and Los Angeles have been the sites of long-running conflicts between black residents and Korean store-owners. Apart from the local issues involved in each case, these conflicts reflect deep concerns of black Americans.

Many blacks are disturbed by the fact that the businesses that profit from their communities are rarely black-owned. They see an urgent need for blacks to take control of their own destiny.

The number of black-owned businesses increased from about 188,000 in 1972 to about 424,000 in 1987. However, only 17 percent of those 424,000 businesses had any paid employees, and fewer than 1 percent had more than 100 employees. While blacks make up slightly more than 12 percent of the nation's population, they own less than 3 percent of the nation's businesses, and black-owned enterprises account for only 1 percent of total business receipts.

Within the African American community there is great
diversity in the voices calling for a dramatic increase in black
entrepreneurship. For example, Louis Farrakhan, the
controversial leader of the Nation of Islam, frequently calls for
blacks to take control of the businesses that depend on their
patronage. Farrakhan envisions a self-sufficient black society,
purified of white influence. Representing a different ideological
viewpoint is Robert L. Woodson, founder of the National Center
for Neighborhood Enterprise and winner of a 1990 "genius
grant" from the MacArthur Foundation. Woodson, who is
harshly critical of many of his former allies in the Civil Rights
movement, has his own vision of community self-sufficiency,
based on a faith in free-market competition and a conviction that
government works most effectively when it helps the poor to help
themselves. Woodson is one of the leading advocates of tenant-
owned public housing.

Unemployment and the Nonworking Poor

Despite gains in the period since the 1960's, blacks remain
underrepresented in many areas of employment. For example,
only 3.2 percent of the nation's lawyers and 3 percent of the
nation's physicians are black.

Far more urgent, though, is the situation of African American
men and women who have no work at all. For several decades,
the rate of black unemployment has been roughly twice as high
as the white rate. In the 1980's, the unemployment rate among
black men frequently reached 20 percent — more than twice the
white rate.

Among young black men, the unemployment rate was even
higher, reaching 49 percent for black teenagers in the 1980's. In
1974, 15.1 percent of black male high school dropouts aged
twenty to twenty-four had not worked at all in the previous year;
by 1986, that figure had increased to 39.7 percent.

Indeed, the unemployment figures, bad as they are, don't
reflect the actual level of black unemployment, because these

Poverty Rates of Persons, by Race: 1969 to 1989

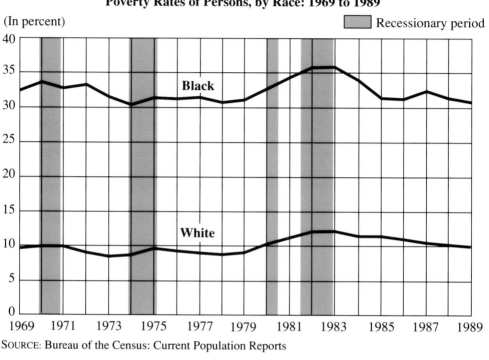

(In percent)   ▨ Recessionary period

SOURCE: Bureau of the Census: Current Population Reports

figures do not include so-called discouraged workers — that is, workers who have stopped looking for a job.

The number of people living in poverty in the United States declined significantly between 1959 and 1989, from thirty-nine million to thirty-two million. However, during that same period black unemployment has increased, and the number of black households headed by single women has risen sharply. As a result, the rate of poverty among blacks is much higher than it is among whites.

Beneath these statistics there is human misery that no statistics can convey. Many people who are classified as poor on the basis of their income move above the poverty level in a year or two. Many people who are temporarily unemployed find work again.

There are others, though, who are chronically poor, chronically unemployed: the so-called underclass, disproportionately black.

Many issues concerning race relations and discrimination arouse strong emotions. (Even the term "underclass" is controversial; those who object to it say that it dehumanizes the people it describes.) That is certainly true of issues connected with poverty, welfare, and the nonworking poor. Very few uncontested statements can be made about black poverty — its causes, its dimensions, and how to lessen its severity.

Many people both inside and outside the black community are dissatisfied with a system that seems to encourage single mothers on welfare to continue to have children with no incentive to get a job. Similarly, many believe that men who are able to work should work. In the 1990's, in part as a result of budget cuts imposed by the recession, many states have enacted or are

A fireman addressing students on career day at a junior high school in Columbus, Ohio.
(Bob Daemmrich/Uniphoto)

considering welfare reforms: "workfare" or "learnfare" programs that encourage welfare recipients to get a job or learn a skill that will enable them to find employment.

Critics of these programs say that states are blaming the poor for economic problems for which they have little responsibility. Critics also charge that threatened cuts in benefits will take families that are affected over the edge into truly desperate poverty and homelessness.

Another contested point is the availability of jobs for unemployed black workers, especially young black men. Advocates of government intervention argue that the government must create new jobs, although to do so would require stiff tax increases. Others, pointing to the steady flow of immigrants who quickly find employment, contend that jobs are already available.

It is difficult to separate unemployment from other problems that grip the black underclass: crime, drugs, AIDS, the breakdown of the family structure. . . . Taken together, these problems — which are brought to our attention daily, hourly, by the media — seem overwhelming. They are indeed formidable, and worthy of national concern. Yet amid this concern we should not lose sight of the millions of African Americans who go to their jobs and come home to their families. Their triumph over discrimination is cause for celebration.

5 Politics and Government

In politics and government African Americans have made some of their most spectacular gains after decades of brutal discrimination. Still, much progress remains to be made to overcome the legacy of slavery and segregation.

Along with all their other rights, slaves had been deprived of the right of citizenship. A series of key amendments to the Constitution changed their legal status and guaranteed the rights of their African American descendants. In 1865, the states ratified the Thirteenth Amendment, abolishing slavery. In 1868, the Fourteenth Amendment was ratified, granting citizenship to all persons born in the United States or naturalized. In 1870, the Fifteenth Amendment was ratified, stating that no citizen could be deprived of the right to vote on the basis of race, color, or previous condition of servitude.

Legally, then, black men had the right to vote. (Women were not granted the right to vote until 1920 when the Nineteenth Amendment was ratified.) In practice, however, it would be a long time before blacks could freely exercise their rights.

In the South, many people were determined to keep blacks in a condition that resembled servitude, even if they were legally free. Segregationists knew that the right to vote was particularly important, and in the period after the Civil War they used any means possible to keep black men from voting: intimidation, beatings, even lynchings. While these violent tactics were still

Black Elected Public Officials, by Type of Office Held, 1970–1989

	Education	Law Enforcement	City & County Offices	US & State Legislatures	Total
1970 (February)	368	213	719	179	1,479
1971 (March)	471	274	909	216	1,870
1972 (March)	676	263	1,112	224	2,275
1973 (April)	777	334	1,268	256	2,635
1974 (April)	804	340	1,607	256	3,007
1975 (April)	951	387	1,885	299	3,522
1976 (April)	1,008	387	2,284	299	4,006
1977 (July)	1,066	415	2,509	316	4,342
1978 (July)	1,154	451	2,616	316	4,544
1979 (July)	1,155	458	2,675	315	4,636
1980 (July)	1,232	491	2,871	326	4,963
1981 (July)	1,293	534	2,914	343	5,109
1982 (July)	1,309	573	3,017	342	5,241
1983 (July)	1,430	620	3,283	386	5,719
1984 (January)	1,445	657	3,367	396	5,865
1985 (January)	1,531	685	3,689	407	6,312
1986 (January)	1,498	676	3,800	410	6,384
1987 (January)	1,542	727	3,949	428	6,646
1988 (January)	1,542	738	4,089	424	6,793
1989 (January)	1,602	759	4,388	441	7,190

SOURCE: U.S. Bureau of the Census, *Statistical Abstract of the United States, 1990,* p. 260, table 436 (data from Joint Center for Political Studies, *Black Elected Officials: A National Roster).* C 3.134:989

NOTES: U.S. and state legislatures includes elected state administrators; city and county officials includes county commissioners and mayors, councilmen, vice-mayors, aldermen, regional officials and others; law enforcement includes judges, magistrates, sheriffs, justices of the peace, and others; education includes members of state education agencies, college boards, school boards, and others.

employed right up to the Civil Rights era, segregationists and white supremacists turned to other tactics as well in order to deny African Americans the right to vote, and thus deny them the right to participate in the democratic government of their own country. Voter registration, for example, was frequently designed to exclude blacks.

One of the key insights of the Civil Rights movement was that laws were already in place guaranteeing blacks an equal status under the Constitution. Black people were determined to claim rights long denied to them—including the right to vote.

Civil Rights workers conducted massive voter registration drives. Many black people, even when they had not been victims of intimidation, had failed to exercise their right to vote because in a segregated society it seemed clear that their voices did not matter. The Civil Rights movement empowered black people and encouraged many of them to take a more active part in the political process.

Unfortunately, many Americans—black and white—remain alienated from the political process. While lower than white totals for registration and voting, black totals are not greatly different. It is a myth that "blacks don't vote." In 1988, for example, a presidential election year, 64.5 percent of the black voting age population reported registration and 51.5 percent reported voting; for whites, the figures were 67.9 percent for registration and 59.1 percent for voting.

Black Gains in Politics and Government

Between 1970 and 1990, the number of black elected officials increased enormously, from under 1,500 in 1970 to more than 7,000 in 1990. As we saw earlier, these gains have been particularly visible in city government, with black mayors currently in office or recently in office in New York, Los Angeles, Chicago, Washington, D.C., Philadelphia, Detroit, Atlanta—virtually all of the major cities of the United States.

Black mayors have been elected in many midsize and smaller cities as well. In the 1980's, for example, Pasadena, California, home of the Rose Bowl, had its first black mayor, Loretta Thompson-Glickman.

The prominence of black leaders in city government is significant in several ways. Mayors of major cities are nationally recognized figures. Their influence paves the way for African Americans to take on even more prominent roles in national politics.

The presence of black leaders in such positions of power tells the black community that their voice counts. Equally important, many of these black city leaders, such as Tom Bradley, the longtime mayor of Los Angeles, have been supported by a substantial percentage of white voters (blacks make up only 14 percent of the population of Los Angeles).

Black city governments affect the entire black community, with benefits that may continue to be felt long after a high-profile mayor is out of office. Typically black city leaders will appoint many black officials to key posts and otherwise use their influence on behalf of their community. This is a time-honored part of the American political process, from which African Americans were long excluded.

Along with those benefits come costs. The administrations of several leading black mayors — most notably Marion Barry of Washington, D.C., whose conviction on cocaine charges culminated several years of scandals — have been marred by corruption and controversy. Some black commentators have suggested that discrimination is at work here — that whites are out to "get" black leaders, or, less dramatically, that black leaders are unfairly being held accountable to higher standards than would be applied to white leaders.

In fact, however, similar scandals involving white administrations — all the way to the presidential level — have been scrutinized with equal intensity. High political visibility brings with it that level of scrutiny. Wherever there is power, there are temptations to abuse it. Most Americans, black and white, know

David Dinkins, the first black mayor of New York City. (James Hamilton)

that. They want honest, responsible leaders; they know that reality will often fall short of the ideal.

Black political gains have not been limited to city government. The campaigns of black leaders such as Jesse Jackson, who sought the Democratic presidential nomination in 1988, and Governor Douglas Wilder of Virginia, the first black governor, who briefly pursued the Democratic presidential nomination in 1992, point the way to the time — perhaps in the not-too-distant future — when an African American will be elected president of the United States.

Inequities and Redistricting

While there have been substantial political gains for blacks, inequities remain. Blacks are not represented in Congress in proportion to their numbers. In 1975, there were fifteen blacks among the 435 members of the House of Representatives; by 1989, the black total had increased to twenty-five. If blacks were represented there roughly in proportion to their numbers, they would have between forty and fifty members. There was one black senator in 1975; in 1989, there were none.

One key to fairness in representation, from the city and county level to the national level, is the way in which the boundaries of political districts are drawn. That process has a profound effect on every aspect of the political life of the nation, but it is largely shaped by political expediency rather than by a genuine quest for fairness.

The number of seats which each state has in the House of Representatives is subject to change every ten years depending on changes in population as registered by the U. S. census. Following the 1990 census, congressional reapportionment is now under way. States that have gained or lost population between 1980 and 1990 must redraw the boundaries of congressional and state legislative districts — a process known as "redistricting."

Redistricting is a political process through and through. The party that is in power in a given state controls the process. If

Republicans are in power, they will shape the boundaries to create as many "safe" districts for Republicans as possible while diluting the impact of Democratic voters. If Democrats are in power, as they are in a majority of state legislatures, they will do the same.

A black district court judge sworn into office in Austin, Texas. (Bob Daemmrich/Uniphoto)

Now, however, another element has been added to the redistricting equation. Black and Hispanic leaders are calling for redistricting that will give them greater representation in state legislatures and in Congress. If the boundaries of a district are drawn in such a way that almost all of the voters within it are black, there is a good chance that a black legislator will be elected from that district. By the same token, if those black voters are divided so that they form part of three different districts, in none of which blacks make up an overwhelming majority (they may share the districts with whites, Hispanics, and other groups), black candidates may not be successful.

The Voting Rights Act

Redistricting is a complex process, and it receives much less attention than many other issues, but it is extremely important. The redistricting battle following the 1990 census is particularly important. To understand some of its implications for African Americans, and for the nation, it is necessary to consider the Voting Rights Act of 1965 and its 1982 amendments.

Earlier we discussed the widespread abuses in the South that prevented or discouraged blacks from voting. The Voting Rights Act of 1965 was designed to curb those abuses. If the percentage of eligible black voters who were registered and who voted in a particular district was disproportionately small, the federal government would intervene. For the most part this legislation had the desired result, and the number of blacks voting in the South increased significantly.

In 1982, Congress passed amendments to the Voting Rights Act that greatly extended its scope. In fact, the impact of these potentially far-reaching changes will be assessed for the first time only after the redistricting following the 1990 census is complete and the court challenges that will follow in turn are settled.

The 1965 Voting Rights Act focused on the electoral *process*, ensuring that blacks could exercise their right to vote without hindrance. In contrast, the 1982 amendments focus on election *results*. According to the 1982 changes, the test of whether minority voters' rights have been protected is "the extent to which members of a protected class have been elected to office in the state or subdivision."

In other words, if redistricting does not produce a certain number of new black and Hispanic seats, there will be court challenges to the new district boundaries. But how many new seats would be required to be in compliance with the law? That remains to be tested in court.

Voter registration drive in Atlanta during the 1988 national Democratic convention. (Paul Conklin/Uniphoto)

Supporters of the 1982 legislation see it as a long-needed remedy to bring about an increase in black representation. Opponents see it as a dangerous precedent, covertly establishing racial quotas for state legislatures and for Congress. This difference in perspective reflects a much larger debate about fairness and the means to achieve it.

6 Crime, Law Enforcement, and the Legal System

Crime is unique among all the problems that trouble Americans today. No other problem cuts across every segment of society. Crime and the fear of crime threaten every American, rich or poor, male or female, young or old, black or white . . . everyone is affected by crime.

In fact, for Americans crime is a national obsession. Crime-related stories grab front-page headlines and dominate local news telecasts. Television dramas and "real-life" shows such as "Cops" and "America's Most Wanted" feed this obsession with crime, as do countless films. A really sensational crime is almost certain to become the subject of a book, a made-for-TV movie, or both — and there is no shortage of sensational crimes.

To a certain extent, these media images of crime reflect a terrible reality: young children struck down in gang crossfire, women battered and killed, defenseless senior citizens murdered for a few dollars. And yet the media images distort reality too. Each year, the Bureau of Justice Statistics releases the National Crime Victimization Survey, which provides an overview of crime in the United States. Between 1973, the first year that statistics were compiled for the survey, and 1990, crimes against individuals decreased by 24.5 percent while crimes against households (such as burglaries and car thefts) decreased by 26.1 percent. Most Americans would be startled by these statistics. The constant barrage of images of crime in the media has led many Americans to believe that crime is steadily increasing. It is true that certain well-publicized categories of violent crime — such as serial killings — *have* increased betwen 1973 and 1990. And, in part because of more stringent laws and more stringent enforcement, crime connected with the sale, possession, and/or use of illegal drugs has increased enormously, clogging court schedules and filling jails and prisons beyond their capacity. Nevertheless, there *has* been not just a small decrease but a very significant decrease in crimes against individuals and against households.

Crime is still a problem, a very serious problem, but exaggerated fears and false ideas about it should not go unchallenged. Here, as in many other areas, we need to think critically about the ways in which our outlook is shaped by the ever-present media.

Crime and the Black Community

What is true of the nation as a whole is even more true of crime and the black community. For African Americans crime is certainly a major problem, and yet, here too, misconceptions and stereotypes have led to distortion.

Although they make up only about 12 percent of the population, blacks constitute a much higher percentage of those arrested for violent crimes such as robbery, rape, and murder. Statistics show that in 1989, blacks made up 65 percent of arrests for robbery, 46.6 percent of arrests for rape, and 56.4 percent of arrests for murder.

Most of the crimes represented in these statistics (though arrest, of course, does not always lead to conviction) were committed by black males. The incidence of crime is particularly high among young black men. According to one widely cited study, 23 percent of black males between the ages of twenty and twenty-nine — that is, almost one in four — are in jail or prison, on probation, or on parole.

Figures such as these, and the toll in wasted lives they represent, have caused some African American leaders to suggest that an entire generation is at risk. Crime reports, reinforced by media images of black criminals, also fuel white fears.

Jail Inmates, 1978–1987

	Black	White	All Races
1978	65,104	89,418	158,394
1983	87,508	130,118	223,552
1984	93,800	138,355	234,500
1985	102,646	151,403	256,615
1986	112,522	159,178	274,444
1987	124,267	168,648	295,873

SOURCE: U.S. Bureau of the Census, *Statistical Abstract of the United States, 1989*, p. 183, table 317 (data from U.S. Bureau of Justice Statistics, *Profile of Jail Inmates, 1978*, and *Jail Inmates [annual]*). C 3.134:989

U.S. Department of Justice, Bureau of Justice Statistics, *Sourcebook of Criminal Justice Statistics, 1988*, p. 606, table 6.26. J 29.9/6:988

NOTES: 'All Races' includes other races not shown separately. Data for 1984–1987 includes juveniles.

Most black men are not criminals. Yet to many white people, the mere presence of a black man is a threat. Black men have described what it is like to feel that in the white world they are always under suspicion.

Lingering racism can be seen in other ways as well. When asked about African Americans and crime, many white people think immediately of blacks as perpetrators of crimes — especially against whites. They are less likely to think of blacks as victims. In fact, however, much black crime is committed against blacks, and blacks are far more likely than whites to be crime victims. In 1991, for example, in Oakland, California, where blacks make up 42.8 percent of the population, 73.8 percent of murder victims were black.

Not all of the misconceptions and distortions concerning this controversial subject can be attributed to whites. Seeing the deathly impact of crime — especially drug-related crime — and AIDS on their community, some black leaders and black journalists have spoken of a white "conspiracy" to destroy blacks. No evidence of such a conspiracy has been presented, and most black people reject the theory. Some, including select community leaders have, however, accepted it.

Earlier, this discussion focused on the need for handling statistics with caution. Articles in newspapers and magazines reporting on the crisis in the black community have sometimes inadvertently given currency to erroneous statistics that make the situation sound worse than it is. For example, an article in *The Christian Science Monitor* (November 5, 1991), based on an interview with C. Eric Lincoln, a highly respected black professor of religion and culture at Duke University, stated that "There are eight black men in jail in the US for every white man." In fact, according to Bureau of Justice statistics, in 1985 there were 260,847 whites in prison and 227,137 blacks. Figures for jail inmates for the same year included 151,403 whites and 102,646 blacks.

Law Enforcement

In March, 1991, millions of Americans watched a video which showed Los Angeles police officers beating a black man, Rodney King, who had been apprehended after a high-speed chase. Repeatedly viewed since that first shocking telecast, the scene has been indelibly etched in the national consciousness.

For black Americans, along with horror at the vicious beating there was also a sense of vindication. Blacks in Los Angeles, and members of other minority groups as well, had been protesting for a long time about police brutality under the administration of Chief Daryl F. Gates. The Rodney King video provided irrefutable proof that their protests were not groundless.

A call for major reform followed the King incident, and in April, 1992, Willie L. Williams, the police commissioner of Philadelphia, was named to succeed the retiring Gates. Williams is the first black man to head the Los Angeles Police Department.

The significance of the Rodney King case wasn't limited to Los Angeles. Many African Americans saw it as an example of a double standard that persists from the days of segregation: one law for whites and another law for blacks.

Many black people believe that discrimination persists not only at the hands of police officers on the street but at every level of the criminal justice system. For example, they argue that more severe sentences are handed out in cases in which the perpetrators are black and the victim is white — such as the case of the Central Park jogger who was brutally assaulted by black youths — than in cases in which the victim is black and the perpetrators are white — such as the Bensonhurst case, in which a black teenager who came to look at a car for sale was shot and killed for "invading" the white neighborhood. Similarly, it is argued that blacks are more likely than whites to be sentenced to the death penalty, even when the circumstances of their crimes are comparable.

"Black life is cheap in the United States," lamented C. Eric Lincoln in the interview cited above. The undervaluing of black life, many African Americans felt, was seen once again in Los Angeles not long after the Rodney King incident. A Korean shopowner, after an altercation with a teenage black girl in which the girl struck the shopowner and knocked her down, shot and killed the girl as she was walking away. Instead of receiving a prison term, the Korean woman was sentenced to community service and probation. The black community in Los Angeles was outraged. Koreans grieved too after unrelated incidents in which Korean shopowners were killed during robberies by black assailants. When the lives of some members of a society are consistently undervalued, ultimately everyone in the society pays the cost.

U.S. park police arrest a crack cocaine dealer in Washington, D.C. (Mark Reinstein/ Uniphoto)

Sometimes that cost can be terribly high. On April 29, 1992, the jury announced its verdict in the trial of four Los Angeles police officers accused of using excessive force in the beating of Rodney King. There were no convictions. Three of the officers were acquitted of all charges, while the jury was deadlocked on the fourth, resulting in a mistrial in his case.

Surprise and outrage greeted the verdict. Shortly after the acquittals were announced, rioting broke out in South Central Los Angeles, quickly spreading to other communities in the greater Los Angeles area. There was widespread looting and destruction. More than fifty people were killed and more than two thousand were injured. Fires set by arsonists struck hundreds of buildings, many of which burned to the ground. Early damage estimates reached $785 million.

The rioting was not confined to the Los Angeles area. While people all over the world watched televised images of the violence in Los Angeles, disturbances broke out in San Francisco, Atlanta, Toronto, Canada, and other cities.

The Rodney King verdict triggered the riots, but more was at stake. While deploring the violence, many black leaders saw it as an expression of frustration with injustice and lack of opportunity. Looking back to the Watts riots of 1965, they asked why, almost thirty years later, conditions for black people in the inner city remain so poor.

Access to Legal Aid

America is a nation of laws. In some ways that is a great strength, as African Americans have shown in turning to the law to demand their rights. The law, however, is not altogether benign. Its power and its intricacy can be used against those who do not have access to its secrets.

Between the 1960's, the era of the Civil Rights movement, and the 1990's, the number of lawyers (and the number of lawsuits) in the United States has grown astronomically. During that time black organizations have skillfully employed the law on behalf of their people. Many individual African Americans, however, lack access to legal aid.

This is not primarily a racial issue but rather a matter of poverty — and thus a problem that disproportionately affects blacks. Today even many middle-class Americans must forgo needed legal aid simply because they cannot afford it. For the poor, the problem is much more acute, as Stephen J. Schulhofer has shown (see Bibliography).

In addition to divorces, child custody disputes, and other family issues, Schulhofer observes, poor people have need of legal aid for many other civil justice cases, just as their middle-class fellow Americans do. Problems relating to discrimination, health care and insurance, utilities — all these and many others frequently call for professional legal assistance. Yet a 1987 survey sponsored by the American Bar Association estimated that poor people obtained professional aid for only 20 percent of their noncriminal legal needs. In part this low figure probably reflects a lack of awareness concerning available legal aid. However, it also reflects a lack of adequate funding for federal programs such as the Legal Services Corporation, which channels money to individual states to provide legal assistance for the poor. During President Ronald Reagan's first term, the budget for the Legal Services Corporation was seriously cut. Despite increased funding from other sources and a restoral of some of the federal cuts, funding throughout the 1980's was not able to keep pace with the steadily increasing cost of providing legal services. As a result, poor people suffered.

Different problems exist in the criminal justice system, where blacks are also disproportionately affected. In the criminal justice system, at least, defendants who cannot afford a lawyer are provided with court-appointed counsel. However, the effectiveness of appointed attorneys varies considerably, and that is a matter of great concern.

The range in effectiveness is not just a matter of individual skill but rather reflects different ways of assigning and compensating court-appointed attorneys. No system of public defenders can guarantee absolute equality in legal assistance, since the most resourceful lawyers will generally be retained by the richest clients. But we should be able to guarantee competent, effective legal representation to everyone, regardless of income.

Black Americans who are struggling with the legal system — who are harassed by the police, unable to afford legal aid, or represented by incompetent or indifferent court-appointed attorneys — are experiencing on a personal scale the great frustration that troubles the black community today: frustration at the gap between legal guarantees of equality and the harsh realities of everyday life.

7 Affirmative Action

"You do not take a person who has been hobbled by chains and liberate him, bring him up to the starting line of a race and then say, 'You are free to compete with all the others,' and still justly believe you have been completely fair."

President Lyndon B. Johnson spoke these words, not long after the passage of the landmark 1964 Civil Rights Act. It was not enough, Johnson said, to ban discriminatory practices in education, employment, and other areas of public life. To move toward equality for all Americans, it was also necessary to make up for past injustices by giving special consideration to those who had been victimized. This was the beginning of what has come to be known as affirmative action.

Of all the policies intended to end discrimination and redress past injustices, those which are placed under the heading of affirmative action are the most far-ranging and the most controversial. Affirmative action policies do not benefit African Americans only; women and members of other minority groups have also benefited and continue to benefit from affirmative action. In this chapter, however, our primary focus will be on affirmative action as it has affected the lives of African Americans.

Righting Wrongs

During World War II, thousands of Japanese American citizens were interned in prison camps at locations throughout the

United States. The United States was at war with Japan, and in the eyes of government authorities anyone of Japanese ancestry was a security risk — although in reality Japanese Americans were overwhelmingly loyal to the United States. The fact that similar measures were not taken against German Americans suggests that there were racist undertones to the internment.

Advocates of affirmative action believe that everyone in our multicultural society should have a fair chance to succeed. (Shaun van Steÿn/Uniphoto)

In 1988, after many years of protest and litigation, Congress passed a Civil Rights Act that provided redress for the injustice done to Japanese Americans. Every living survivor of the internment is to receive a one-time payment of $20,000 from the U.S. government. It is estimated that the total cost of reparations, which did not actually begin until 1990, will reach $1.2 billion. Although these payments will not truly compensate victims of the internment for the substantial losses they suffered, both spiritual and material, the payments acknowledge the injustice done to

Japanese Americans and offer a small but significant sum in redress.

In 1992, Leonard Jeffries, Jr., the controversial professor of Afro-American Studies at New York's City College, argued that the U.S. government should pay reparations to African Americans and Native Americans. If, as most Americans believe, it was right to compensate Japanese Americans for the injustice they suffered, are not black Americans and Native Americans entitled to much more substantial compensation, in proportion to the extreme and prolonged injustice to which they were subjected?

As yet, there has not been widespread support for Jeffries' proposal. The principle behind it, though, is the basis for affirmative action. Everyone — everyone except extreme racists — agrees that black Americans have historically been the victims of monstrous injustice. To a degree impossible to calculate precisely, the conditions in which many black Americans live today are directly traceable to past injustice. The question is what to do about it. How is fairness to be achieved?

Preferences Versus Quotas

In 1964, blacks were excluded from skilled labor positions in most industries, and black supervisors were even more rare. Following the passage of the Civil Rights Act, which he had strongly supported, President Johnson issued an executive order instructing businesses with federal government contracts to take "affirmative action" in hiring blacks and members of other minority groups. In this way the president sent a message to *all* companies in the United States — not just federal contractors.

Some companies did not really try to comply with the 1964 Civil Rights Act and the presidential order that followed it. There was uncertainty about the new law, which was only partly resolved by several major Supreme Court decisions that broadly reaffirmed the principle of affirmative action.

Meanwhile, however, many employers had begun active recruitment of African Americans for positions from which they had been excluded in the past. In addition, black workers who had formerly been stuck in low-level jobs were given training that made them eligible for promotion.

In both hiring and promotion, black workers were generally competing with white workers. To follow the principle of affirmative action — that is, to make up at least in part for past injustices — many employers used racial preference as a guide in making decisions about hiring and promotion. Given two applicants, one black and one white, more or less equally qualified, they would hire the black applicant. In some cases, if they were to pursue affirmative action to any meaningful extent, employers would have to hire or promote black workers in preference to white workers who were clearly *more* qualified.

The term "racial preferences," then, simply means that, along with all the other factors which an employer takes into account in evaluating a candidate for hiring or promotion — for example, educational background, performance in an interview and/or on standardized tests, previous job-performance — race is figured into the equation, sometimes decisively, sometimes not.

Racial quotas, in contrast, establish fixed numerical goals which employers are required or strongly urged to meet. For example, managers in a national retail chain might be told that within a year, a certain percentage of their department supervisors must be minorities, a certain percentage women, and so on. The advantage of quotas is that they give employers definite goals to shoot for while establishing a standard by which compliance to affirmative action policies can be measured.

Quotas have serious drawbacks as well, however — drawbacks that make them very controversial and that cause many businesses and institutions to avoid explicit numerical goals. In the past, quotas have been used as a tool of discrimination. At one time, many universities and graduate schools limited the number of Jewish students they accepted. If the schools had judged candidates solely on the basis of academic achievement, many more Jewish students would have been admitted. Today, many Asian American students believe that they are the victims of similar quotas.

Whenever businesses and institutions are forced to fulfill racial quotas in hiring and promotion, there is a danger that race will override all other considerations. In many fields, there are plenty of well-qualified black employees who, in the past, would have been excluded on the basis of race. In other fields, however, there may not be enough qualified black candidates to fulfill the desired racial balance. In such fields, long-term changes are needed to create a pool of qualified black candidates — not the quick fix provided by affirmative action.

Reverse Discrimination

While racial quotas provoke the strongest criticism, many Americans disapprove of racial preferences in other forms as well. Attitudes toward affirmative action policies tend to divide along racial lines, according to several national polls recently conducted by different organizations. Acknowledging that there was a need for affirmative action at the time of the Civil Rights movement, many whites believe that after thirty years such policies have served their purpose and should not be continued; in contrast, a majority of blacks believe that affirmative action should continue to be pursued vigorously. Among neither whites nor blacks, it should be noted, is there anything approaching unanimous agreement on this issue.

For example, *The Christian Science Monitor* (April 10, 1992) reported the results of a poll which asked "Should employers give special consideration to minority job applicants in order to increase the number of minority employees?" Among whites the response to this question was strongly negative: 27 percent of whites polled answered yes while 60 percent answered no. In contrast, 65 percent of blacks polled answered yes while 19 percent answered no.

Many whites who object to affirmative action policies argue that these policies frequently result in "reverse discrimination." A case that was heard by the Supreme Court in 1976, *Franks v. Bowman Transportation Company, Inc.*, illustrates the conflict over reverse discrimination. At issue in this case was the granting of "retroactive seniority" to black workers. Eligibility for promotion and benefits is frequently tied to seniority. Black workers hired under the impetus of affirmative action were at a disadvantage, since their previous exclusion made it impossible for them to accumulate seniority as they would have done under a fair system. To make up for this disadvantage, black workers at Bowman were granted retroactive seniority.

White workers objected to this policy, saying that it forced them to pay for past injustices for which they were not personally responsible and over which they had no control. A majority of the Court, however, upheld the granting of retroactive seniority to black workers, who were thus eligible for promotion and benefits before white workers hired at the same time.

Certainly this case — and many others like it which could be cited — could be described as an instance of reverse discrimination. What critics of affirmative action generally fail to provide, however, is an explanation of how the injustices of slavery and segregation might in part be redressed *without* cost to whites who are not historically responsible for past discrimination.

A more difficult question is when that debt will be paid — how long must affirmative action be continued? The answer to this question is complicated by the fact that African Americans have to share the demand for affirmative action resources with an increasingly diverse population — Hispanics, Asians, and immigrants from throughout the world as the United States experiences its largest wave of immigration since the first decades of the twentieth century.

Affirmative action policies have brought greater diversity to college campuses. (Ron Sherman/Uniphoto)

Higher Education

One area in which affirmative action policies have been particularly prominent is higher education. At every level, from two-year community colleges to elite universities, institutions of higher education have sought to increase black enrollment.

Many state colleges and universities have stated that their goal is for the racial and gender makeup of their student body to approximate the makeup of the population they serve. According to such a policy, for a state in which 20 percent of the population is black, for example, roughly 20 percent of the students at state colleges and universities should be black.

In general such goals have not been translated into rigidly enforced quotas. Still, they have led to controversy. At the University of California at Berkeley, for example, the most prestigious campus in the University of California system, highly qualified white and Asian American students have been denied admission in favor of minority students with significantly lower grades and test-scores. As noted earlier, Asian Americans, who already make up more than 25 percent of the student body at Berkeley, believe that their numbers would be even higher were it not for quotas that discriminate against them.

Private colleges and universities have also made an effort to increase black enrollment. This is true not only of elite universities which draw students from throughout the United States and urban institutions which draw on a large local black population but also of smaller colleges, many of which are located in areas where very few blacks live.

Colleges and universities implement affirmative action policies in various ways. One is active recruitment of black high school graduates. Another is to add race to the list of factors used in evaluating students for admission. In addition, schools may lower admissions standards in order to accept black applicants and applicants from other minority groups.

It is this last policy that has provoked the most controversy regarding affirmative action in higher education. Schools want to make up for the injustices of the past, when black students were restricted to segregated institutions or — as was usually the case — denied higher education altogether. As a result, they admit black students whose educational background is not comparable to that of many of their fellow students. Critics of this policy argue that it does black students a disservice. Those who enter unqualified for college work are likely to fail, while those who enter with excellent preparation will unfairly be seen by many of their peers as less than qualified.

Supporters of this policy contend that colleges and universities can do much more to help black students once they have been admitted. Despite the high drop-out rate, affirmative action has made it possible for many black students to receive a college education. For the children of these black college graduates, the step from high school to college will be easier than it was for their parents.

As African American activists have long argued, affirmative action has always played a part in American higher education — "affirmative action" for the rich, whose sons and daughters have taken their appointed places at Harvard and Yale and other elite institutions. Affirmative action for blacks and other minorities is an attempt to balance the scale.

8 Visions and Values

In the 1990's, probably more so than at any time since the 1960's, there is intense public concern over racial issues in the United States — particularly issues that involve African Americans. Television specials, movies, newspaper and magazine articles, books, fiction and nonfiction alike, all explore the ongoing struggle for equality, the troubled state of race relations, and the crisis conditions within black inner-city communities.

In these stories and studies, we frequently encounter statements such as this: "blacks believe that . . ." or "whites feel that . . ." or "unlike blacks, whites . . ." Generalizations about how blacks or whites think about this or that issue may be necessary at times for the purposes of discussion. We should be wary of such generalizations, though, for if we fall into the habit of accepting them too readily we'll be guilty of a form of racism.

All African Americans don't think alike, nor do all whites, or Chinese Americans, or members of any other racial or ethnic group. As human beings we all live in the same world, but we don't see that world in the same way. Different visions reflect different value-systems or worldviews. Within the black community many different worldviews exist, some largely in agreement though differing in certain ways, some sharply antagonistic.

This diversity of viewpoints has not been well-reported in most media accounts of the black community. In part the problem is ignorance: Whites who are writing about racial issues often lack a firsthand, in-depth knowledge of the black community. At the same time, when dealing with white society, blacks have tended to minimize the differences and disagreements within their own community.

It is easy to understand why. From the time of slavery, African Americans have been an embattled community, a people under attack. Well-publicized divisions within their community could

Martin Luther King Memorial in Atlanta, Georgia. (Justin K. Anderson)

be exploited by their oppressors. Today, however, many black thinkers are questioning this code of public solidarity, arguing that blacks must be free to differ with and even strongly criticize other blacks without being ostracized as traitors to their race.

Name any issue that confronts African Americans, and you will be able to find within the black community many different approaches to that problem. In this chapter we will touch on just two of the viewpoints or worldviews that are influential among black Americans today, both of which can be seen in part as responses to racism and discrimination. We'll also briefly discuss the ideal of integration: Is it still alive?

The Black Church

The black church was born out of suffering. African Americans were introduced to Christianity during the period of slavery. Like many other oppressed peoples in other times and other places, they found in Christianity a refuge from their daily misery and hope for a better future.

African Americans did not simply copy the practices of white churchgoers. They brought to Christianity spiritual inclinations shaped by African religious traditions. They created their own forms of worship and their own music. Most popular music in America today has roots in the black church.

After slavery was abolished, black churches led the way in educating former slaves and establishing black colleges (see chapter 3). In the decades that followed, the church continued to play a central role in the lives of African Americans. Church was the place where everyone met. In part because of segregation and limited job opportunities, a very high percentage of black college graduates entered the ministry (see chapter 4). The ministry also attracted many gifted African Americans who were not formally educated but who were natural leaders in their communities.

In the 1950's and 1960's, the black church contributed significantly to the Civil Rights movement, through organizations such as the Southern Christian Leadership Conference, through outstanding leaders such as Martin Luther King, Jr. (who was an ordained Baptist minister), and above all through the participation of countless individual churches and their congregations.

The vitality of the black church continues in the 1990's. In fact, several of the largest and fastest-growing churches in the United States are black congregations led by black ministers. Yet the church, like the black community as a whole, must struggle with deep-seated social problems. Less widely publicized than initiatives by politicians or celebrities, efforts to address the needs of an endangered generation are being carried out by black churchpeople from many different denominations.

While the black church remains influential, some African Americans strongly believe that Christianity has had a negative impact on their community. Their criticisms are many. They mourn the loss of African traditions. They note the hypocrisy of the white slaveowners who considered themselves Christians while treating other people as if they were less than human. They suggest that much in the black church is inauthentic, imposed by force on African Americans and inherited to this day. Some critics draw a connection between Christianity and the "colonialist mentality" of Europeans who enslaved Africans and decimated the native population of America.

Of course, in the black community as in the white community there are many people who don't consistently practice any religion. Among blacks who are seeking an alternative to Christianity, however, some have turned to Islam.

The Nation of Islam

Muslims make up about one-half of 1 percent of the U. S. population, or about 1.4 million people. Of that number, 40 percent are black. Only about 2 percent of the approximately thirty million blacks in the United States are Muslims.

Although Muslims make up only a small percentage of African Americans, they are more visible nationally than their numbers might suggest. They include the group known as the Nation of Islam (often referred to in the 1960's as Black Muslims), to which Malcolm X was converted in the 1950's and from which he broke in the 1960's to align himself with mainstream Islam.

Founded in Detroit in the early 1930's, the Nation of Islam taught that African Americans were lost descendants of Muslims. The doctrines of this faith as promulgated by its leader, Elijah Muhammad, combined orthodox Muslim beliefs with ideas not to be found in the Koran, the sacred book of Islam. Elijah Muhammad taught that white people are "devils," created inferior to blacks.

Elijah Muhammad died in 1975 and was succeeded by his son, W. Deen Muhammad, who wished to unite with mainstream Islam as Malcolm X had done before his assassination. This also would have meant admitting white Muslims to membership. As a result, there was a split in 1977. The remaining faction, which included those who did not follow W. Deen Muhammad, was led by Minister Louis Farrakhan.

Members of the Nation of Islam are expected to adhere to a strict moral code while keeping themselves separate from the corruptions of white society. They are instructed to abstain from alcoholic beverages and to follow other regulations concerning diet and dress. Farrakhan teaches self-discipline and economic self-sufficiency for blacks (see chapter 4). Like Leonard Jeffries, he has suggested that the United States should pay reparations to African Americans for injustices they have suffered.

Widely criticized for his anti-Semitic statements, Farrakhan has spoken to large audiences throughout the United States. Many of his listeners, while not ready to commit themselves to the Nation of Islam, respond very positively to his emphasis on black self-sufficiency and to his scathing attacks on whites and their culture.

Louis Farrakhan. (John Neubauer)

A Color-Blind Society?

The black church and the Nation of Islam differ from each other in many respects, but in one important respect they are similar: Both are black organizations, not integrated. The black church, of course, is not anti-white. Black clergy regularly work in cooperation with white colleagues. Some predominantly black congregations include white members, just as some predominantly white congregations include black members. Nevertheless, the black church is largely black and the white church is largely white.

One of the foremost goals of the Civil Rights movement was a truly "color-blind" society — a society in which every one would be seen as an individual, in which the color of one's skin wouldn't matter any more than the color of one's hair. That was the ideal behind integration. Now, thirty years later, we're clearly far from achieving a color-blind society. Is the ideal of integration dead?

On some university campuses, black students live in all-black dormitories — not segregated against their will but by choice. Elementary and secondary schools in Washington, D.C., Atlanta, Detroit, Chicago, Cleveland, Indianapolis, Portland, Oregon, and other cities have adopted "Afrocentric" curricular programs that encourage African American students to identify themselves with Africa and that make sweeping claims for the African cultural heritage.

There are situations in which the ideal of integration appears to have been fulfilled. Black people and white people work smoothly together, under fire on the battlefield or in the more mundane routines of the office or the factory. Maybe, then, the ideal is not dead; it just needs to be redefined.

Perhaps for many African Americans a color-blind society is not a high priority. (What would such a society be like? No one knows. It's never been achieved.) But equality? Yes, *that* is a high priority. Fairness, yes. An end to discrimination, subtle as well as blatant, yes. Justice, yes.

9 Some Who Made a Difference

Throughout their history, African Americans have been blessed with inspiring leaders. Dynamic figures such as Martin Luther King, Jr., and Malcolm X have made a significant impact not only in the black community but throughout American society. Thanks to programs such as Black History Month and textbooks that for the first time acknowledge black contributions to American history, students of all races are learning about earlier black leaders such as Ida B. Wells (1862-1931), who courageously crusaded against lynching in the South at a time when blacks who challenged the white power-structure were risking their lives.

Many of the people who have contributed to the African American struggle for equality will never be studied in history books. A black man who refused to accept job discrimination even though to fight it meant hostility from coworkers and years of exhausting litigation, a black woman who worked with preschool children in the Head Start program, a black student who excelled academically even though it meant being cut off from neighborhood friends — people such as these, nameless so far as history is concerned, have worked in countless ways to overcome discrimination and the crushing disadvantages imposed on many African Americans.

This chapter highlights the contributions of four African Americans. Many others could have been mentioned as well. No

Martin Luther King, Jr. (Library of Congress)

one of these four should be seen as representing all black
people — an unfair burden to place on anyone. As we noted in the
previous chapter, there are diverse viewpoints within the black
community just as there are in any other community.

Different as they are from one another, these four do have
something in common. All of them have changed people's minds.
All of them have challenged preconceptions about African
Americans. In doing so, they have attacked prejudice and
discrimination at the source.

═══════════════

Rosa Parks

Rosa Parks (1913-   ) became a powerful symbol for the
Civil Rights movement when she refused to give up her seat on a
bus to a white man in Montgomery, Alabama, on December 1,
1955.

Parks was born Rosa McCauley in Tuskegee, Alabama; her
father was a carpenter and her mother was a teacher. When she
was a young girl, her father left the family; Rosa, her mother,
and her younger brother moved to her grandparents' farm. She
was educated at the Montgomery Industrial School for Girls and
at Alabama State College.

Long before the bus incident, Parks and her husband,
Raymond, a barber, had been active in the NAACP, working for
equal rights for blacks. At the time of the bus incident she was
employed as a seamstress at a Montgomery department store.

In the mid-1950's, blacks made up 70 percent of the ridership
on Montgomery's city buses. The first few rows of every bus,
however, were reserved for whites, and even when those sections
were empty blacks were to remain in the rear of the bus, standing
if necessary. If the white section was full and another white
person boarded the bus, a black person who was already seated
was expected to give up his or her seat to the white rider.

That was what happened on December 1, 1955. Rosa Parks
and three other blacks sitting in the same row were told to give

up their seats so that a white man could sit in the row. The other three complied, but Parks refused. She was arrested and freed on bail.

Downplaying her courage, Parks later said that she was simply too tired that day to get up from her seat. Her bravery and determination allowed the NAACP to begin a court challenge to the unfair system in Montgomery. Meanwhile, Martin Luther King, Jr., and other black leaders came to Montgomery. They organized a massive boycott of the city bus system, which suffered financially without black riders. The boycott lasted 382 days until the Supreme Court, having ruled in 1956 that such segregation was unconstitutional, ordered Montgomery to cease segregated seating on the city buses.

The Montgomery bus boycott first brought King to national prominence. This key moment in the Civil Rights movement focused attention throughout the United States on a system that had long been accepted in the South as a way of life. But Rosa Parks said no, and suddenly the grotesque unfairness and the sheer absurdity of segregation were exposed to the nation.

For Parks and her family, the cost of her action was great. She lost her job, while her husband, as a result of intense stress, became unable to work. In 1957, the Parkses moved to Detroit, where Rosa continued to participate in community service. In 1965, she began her long tenure working in the office of Democratic Congressman John Conyers, Jr., who established a strong record on Civil Rights issues. Active well past retirement age, Parks has been widely honored for her contributions.

─────────────

James P. Comer

James P. Comer (1934-   ) is a child psychiatrist whose theory of education, known as the Comer Method, has led to substantial gains in achievement for black children at schools where it has been implemented.

Education, as we saw in chapter 3, is one of the chief concerns of the black community. There is complete agreement only on

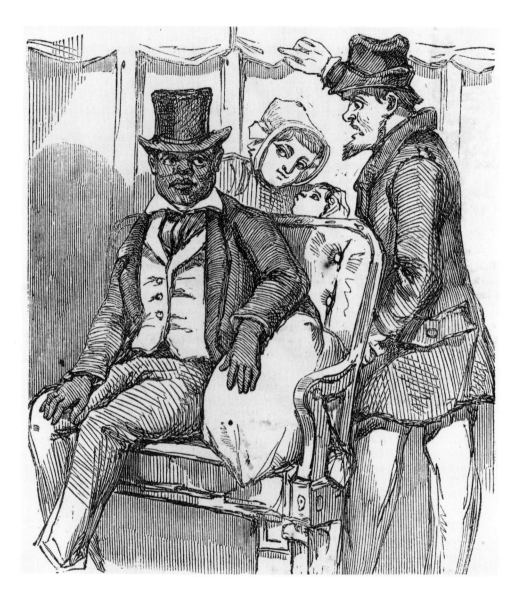

When Rosa Parks said no to the white man who expected her to give up her seat, she was speaking for generations of black victims of discrimination. (Library of Congress)

one point — that education for black students needs to be improved at every level. Beyond that, there are a host of competing theories explaining why things are the way they are now and how they could be improved.

Comer's approach to these problems begins with the importance of self-esteem, which is vital to the success of all children, whatever their race. This emphasis reflects his own childhood experience. Comer was born in East Chicago, Indiana, one of five children; his father was a laborer in a steel mill, and his mother was a domestic who had only one year of formal schooling. Despite their limited education and the discrimination they encountered daily in their difficult and unrewarding jobs, Comer's parents instilled in him and his siblings a strong sense that they were valued as individuals and that they were capable of high achievement. Many of the neighborhood children he grew up with, Comer has recalled, lacked that kind of encouragement, and many of them are now destitute, or dead, or in jail.

Comer himself went on to a distinguished academic career. For many years he has headed Yale University's Child Study Center; he is also Associate Dean of Yale Medical School and professor of psychiatry. Yet he has not forgotten where he came from. He has devoted his professional life to helping black children achieve their full potential.

When children begin school, Comer believes, teachers must convince them that school is a place where they will be valued. At the same time, while building the students' self-esteem, teachers must set goals for them that are attainable but challenging.

The Comer Method, like any educational theory, has its critics. Some critics, for example, argue that Comer places too much emphasis on self-esteem and not enough on poverty and other material social conditions that affect the academic performance of black children. Nevertheless, the Comer Method has produced dramatic gains for inner-city black children in New Haven, Connecticut, the school system where it has been most extensively applied, and at other locations as well. As a result, in

1990 the Rockefeller Foundation funded a five-year, $15-million
program to implement the Comer Method at eight schools
scattered throughout the United States; if the program is
successful, other schools will be added.

Comer believes that many well-intentioned remedial programs
for black students reflect white society's unconscious assumption
that blacks really aren't capable of high academic achievement.
And, he adds, many black students have internalized this false
belief, causing them to doubt and undervalue themselves. What
most black children need, Comer believes, is not remedial
education but education based on respect and full understanding
of the student as a person.

Haki R. Madhubuti

Haki R. Madhubuti (1942-   ) is a writer and publisher who
has reached a market in the black community largely ignored by
mainstream publishers.

Haki Madhubuti was born Don L. Lee in Little Rock,
Arkansas. He attended Dunbar Vocational High School in
Chicago. After serving in the army from 1960 to 1963, he
continued his education at Chicago's City College, Roosevelt
University, and the University of Illinois, Chicago Circle. During
this period he held several jobs, including work as an apprentice
curator at the Du Sable Museum of African American History
from 1963 to 1967.

The Civil Rights movement built bridges between blacks and
whites, but it also unleashed a great deal of black rage—rage that
had been supressed under slavery and segregation. The
accumulated anger at centuries of injustice exploded in race riots,
in campus demonstrations, in radical political movements (such
as the Black Panthers), and in many other forms.

Madhubuti, whose first book of poems was published in 1967,
still under the name Don Lee, was one of many young black
writers of the 1960's to express that rage; the title of his third

volume of poems, published in 1969, was *Don't Cry, Scream*. His poetry from the 1960's and early 1970's uses language like a blunt instrument. Defying the norms of Standard English, these poems employ slang, obscenities, street language, deliberately breaking rules of spelling and punctuation. The tone of the poems is consistently angry, with harsh denunciations of whites and white society. In 1973, when he adopted the name Haki R. Madhubuti, a new tone entered his work, as he sought to use poetry as a medium for teaching Muslim values.

Unlike many contemporary poets, Madhubuti had always seen poetry as a tool for social change. In 1967, the same year his first collection was published, he founded Third World Press. Through this outlet he has published not only his own books — including many works of nonfiction as well as poetry — but also books by other black writers.

According to a story in *Publishers Weekly* (January 20, 1992), based on an interview with Madhubuti, his sixteen books have sold a total of more than one million copies. Madhubuti's recent book *Black Men: Obsolete, Single, Dangerous? Afrikan-American Families in Transition* has been a best-seller in the black community, even though it has not appeared on national best-seller lists. In addition to his writing and publishing, Madhubuti, a professor at Chicago State University, is involved in elementary education and directs a small chain of African American bookstores.

One of the many widely accepted myths about African Americans is that "black people don't buy books." Yet Third World Press reports sales of more than one million copies for a single title, Chancellor Williams' *The Destruction of Black Civilization*. First published in the 1970's, Williams' book continues to be among the leading sellers at many African American bookstores. Haki Madhubuti has amply demonstrated that there is a market in the black community for books written and published by blacks.

Endesha Ida Mae Holland

Endesha Ida Mae Holland (1945-   ) has told her life-story in *From the Mississippi Delta*, a play that has special resonance for women — a story of hardship and tragedy, but also of unexpected good fortune and adversity overcome.

Endesha Ida Mae Holland was born in Greenwood, Mississippi. Her mother ran a so-called rooming house that was actually a house of prostitution. Raped at the age of eleven, Holland dropped out of school in ninth grade; before long she herself was working as a prostitute.

The first of several dramatic changes of direction in her life came in 1963, when she became involved with the Civil Rights movement. Without planning to, Holland suddenly became a Civil Rights activist. The organization she joined, the Student Nonviolent Coordinating Committee (SNCC), was doing voter registration in Mississippi. White authorities were trying to limit registration of black voters. Along with other SNCC members, Holland was arrested a number of times.

In 1965, Holland's mother died in a fire that consumed their house. No arrests were made in the case, but Holland believed that the fire had been set by white racists who had intended to kill her. Desperate, she contacted people in Minnesota whom she had met on a SNCC fund-raising tour. They offered her a place to stay.

Involved with black student groups and community organizations in Minnesota, Holland attended college part-time. In 1985, she received a Ph.D. from the University of Minnesota, and she now teaches at the State University of New York at Buffalo.

In *From the Mississippi Delta*, which opened Off Broadway in 1991 after successful performances at several regional theaters, Holland recounts this extraordinary story in dramatic form. Her play testifies to the ability of black people to overcome poverty and abuse. It shows, too, that professional and artistic success —

personal fulfillment — doesn't require a person to give up his or her commitment to the community. Finally, to women of all races, many of whom have been victimized as Holland was and many of whom know what it is like to combine education and career with other responsibilities, Holland's improbable story is deeply encouraging.

10 Time Line

1619   A group of twenty Africans arrives in Virginia as indentured servants.

1659   The first laws dealing with fugitive slaves are passed.

1664   An act requiring all non-Christian servants to serve for life marks the beginning of a chain of legislation which builds the institution of slavery in the United States.

1667   The British Parliament adopts a set of codes to regulate slaves on British plantations. These set the ground for the slave codes.

1712   Twenty-three armed slaves mount an insurrection in New York City and twenty-one are executed.

1739   The Stono Rebellion, a full-scale uprising against slavery in North Carolina, ends in more than 70 deaths.

1741   A rumor spreads that blacks and poor whites are uniting to take over New York City. The city offers rewards for names and then arrests 200 blacks and whites. Thirty-one blacks and four whites are executed.

1776   By the end of the Revolutionary War, more than 5,000 blacks had fought on the American side.

1780   Pennsylvania becomes the first state to abolish slavery.

1787   Congress includes a provision in the Northwest
       Ordinance that there would be no slavery in territories.

1805   Vermont Senator Bradley introduces a bill to prohibit
       the slave trade. Consideration of the bill is postponed.

1807   The law prohibiting the African slave trade is passed.

1810   The Underground Railroad begins. Over the next fifty
       years it enables as many as 100,000 slaves to escape to
       freedom.

1831   Following the rebellions of Denmark Vesey and Nat
       Turner, slave codes are expanded, including mandatory
       illiteracy and the outlawing of assembly without a white
       present.

1850   The Fugitive Slave Law is passed, requiring
       northerners to return fugitive slaves to their owners.
       Free blacks are in danger of being falsely accused of
       being runaways.

1857   The Dred Scott case decides that slaves have "no rights
       that a white man need respect."

1861   Many blacks are not allowed to join the northern war
       effort while the Confederates employ their slaves in
       their fight to secede. By the end of the Civil War, more
       than 156,000 blacks had fought for the Union Army.

1863   President Lincoln announces the Emancipation
       Proclamation.

1865   The Thirteenth Amendment is passed, ending 200 years
       of slavery.

1866   Congress passes the Civil Rights Act, which gives
       former slaves citizenship.

1868   With passage of the Fourteenth Amendment, black men are given voting rights.

1876   The Deal of 1876 marks the beginning of Jim Crow legislation.

1896   All but one judge in the case of *Plessy v. Ferguson* rule that the establishment of "separate but equal" facilities is constitutional.

1920   With passage of the Nineteenth Amendment, women are given the right to vote.

1945   A New York state law against discrimination is the first modern Equal Employment Opportunity law.

1954   In *Brown v. Topeka Board of Education* the Supreme Court reverses *Plessy v. Ferguson* and rules for desegregation in public schools.

1955   The Montgomery bus boycott begins.
       Supreme Court orders school districts to implement desegregation "with all deliberate speed."

1956   Supreme Court rules that segregated seating on buses is unconstitutional.

1960   Four black students sit at a segregated lunch counter in Greensboro, North Carolina, and refuse to move; soon throughout the South, civil rights groups are preaching nonviolent resistance to segregation and discrimination.

1961   Freedom Riders organized by the Congress of Racial Equality (CORE) travel by bus from Washington, D.C., to test desegregation in Southern bus stations; many of them are attacked and/or arrested.

1963 Civil rights activist Medgar Evers is assassinated
      outside his home in Jackson, Mississippi.
      Between 200,000 and 300,000 people participate in the
      "March on Washington," gathering at the Lincoln
      Memorial to protest against continuing racial
      discrimination.

1964 Congress passes a major Civil Rights Act, strongly
      supported by President Lyndon Johnson; this act, which
      mandates equality of opportunity, initiates affirmative
      action policies.
      Martin Luther King, Jr., receives the Nobel Peace
      Prize.
      Three civil rights workers, James Chaney, Michael
      Schwerner, and Andrew Goodman, are murdered in
      Philadelphia, Mississippi; although several arrests are
      made, no one is convicted of the crime.
      Rioting in Harlem sets a pattern to be followed in black
      inner-city communities over the next several years.

1965 Martin Luther King, Jr., leads a march from Selma,
      Alabama, to Montgomery, the state capital, to protest
      the ongoing attempt by white segregationists to deny
      blacks their voting rights.
      Malcolm X is assassinated in New York by three
      members of the Nation of Islam.
      Congress passes the Voting Rights Act, intended to
      ensure blacks of the right to vote.
      Rioting in the black community of Watts in Los
      Angeles.

1966 The Black Panther Party is founded in Oakland,
      California.
      Stokely Carmichael, head of the Student Nonviolent
      Coordinating Committee (SNCC), proclaims the
      doctrine of "black power."

1967   Thurgood Marshall is named as a justice of the Supreme Court, the first black appointed to the nation's highest court.
Rioting in Newark, New Jersey, Detroit, Buffalo, and other cities.
Carl Stokes elected mayor of Cleveland.
Richard Hatcher elected mayor of Gary, Indiana.

1968   Martin Luther King, Jr., is assassinated in Memphis, Tennessee, by a white man, James Earl Ray.
Shirley Chisholm is elected to the U.S. House of Representatives from New York, becoming the first black woman in Congress.

1970   Supreme Court orders the Memphis school system to implement desegregation, reaffirming the principles stated in 1954 in *Brown v. Topeka Board of Education*.

1973   Tom Bradley elected mayor of Los Angeles.
Maynard Jackson elected mayor of Atlanta.
Coleman Young elected mayor of Detroit.

1974   In Boston, the beginning of busing to bring about school desegregation prompts protests, boycotts, and violence.

1976   Supreme Court prohibits private schools from excluding black students on the basis of race.

1977   Andrew Young appointed as U.S. Ambassador to the United Nations.
The television miniseries "Roots," based on the book by Alex Haley, presents the African American experience in dramatic form; the widely viewed miniseries sweeps the Emmy awards.

1979   Andrew Young resigns as U.S. Ambassador to the United Nations after an unauthorized meeting with a representative of the Palestine Liberation Organization.

1982   Amendments to the reaffirmed Voting Rights Act of
       1965 shift emphasis from the electoral process (ensuring
       that the right to vote is not impeded) to election results
       (are minorities represented proportionately?), with far-
       reaching implications for redistricting.

1983   Federal holiday in honor of Martin Luther King, Jr.,
       established, to begin in 1986.
       Supreme Court rules that private schools which practice
       racial discrimination are not elegible for federal tax
       exemptions.
       Harold Washington elected mayor of Chicago.
       W. Wilson Goode elected mayor of Philadelphia.

1986   Martin Luther King Day is celebrated for the first time.
       A black man, Michael Griffith, is hit by a car and
       killed while trying to escape from white assailants in
       Howard Beach, a section of Queens, New York.

1989   Louis Sullivan named Secretary of Health and Human
       Services.
       Colin Powell named Chairman of the U.S. Joint Chiefs
       of Staff.
       David Dinkins elected mayor of New York City.
       L. Douglas Wilder elected governor of Virginia,
       becoming the nation's first black governor.
       A black teenager, Yusef Hawkins, is shot and killed in
       the largely white Brooklyn community of Bensonhurst.

1991   The Civil Rights Act of 1991, reversing the trend
       established by several recent Supreme Court decisions,
       makes it easier for victims of job discrimination to
       prove their case and allows them to claim
       compensatory and punitive damages.

1992   The trial of four Los Angeles policemen accused of
       excessive force in the beating of Rodney King in

March, 1991, ends with acquittal for three of the
defendants and a mistrial for one; the day the verdicts
are announced, rioting breaks out in Los Angeles.

11 Resources

A. Philip Randolph Institute
260 Park Ave., S., 6th Fl.
New York, NY 10010
(212) 533-8000
   Founded in 1964 by the black labor leader for which it is
named, the institute emphasizes cooperation between organized
labor and the black community.

American Association for Affirmative Action
11 E. Hubbard St., Suite 200
Chicago, IL 60611
(312) 329-2512
   Founded in 1974, this organization seeks to encourage the
implementing of affirmative action programs and equal
opportunity in employment; also serves as a liaison with federal,
state, and local agencies concerned with compliance with
affirmative action policies.

Association for the Study of Afro-American Life and History
1407 14th St., N.W.
Washington, D.C. 20005
(202) 667-2822
   Founded in 1915, this organization promotes the study of black
history and culture through a wide variety of programs. Publishes
a scholarly journal, the quarterly *Journal of Negro History*.

Congress of Racial Equality
1457 Flatbush Ave.

Brooklyn, NY 11210
(718) 434-3580

Founded in 1942, CORE derives its black nationalist program from the pan-African philosophy of Marcus Garvey; emphasizes self-sufficiency and fosters awareness of the African heritage of black Americans.

National Association for the Advancement of Colored People
4805 Mt. Hope Dr.
Baltimore, MD 21215
(212) 481-4100

Founded in 1909, and with a current membership exceeding 400,000, the NAACP is the preeminent African American organization. It publishes a journal, *Crisis* (ten issues/year) and an annual report.

National Urban League
500 E. 62nd St.
New York, NY 10021
(212) 310-9000

Founded in 1910, the NUL is one of the nation's leading civil rights organizations, committed to equality for black Americans and other minorities.

Southern Christian Leadership Conference
335 Auburn Ave., N.E.
Atlanta, GA 30312
(404) 522-1420

Founded in 1957, the SCLC is a nonsectarian agency that combats prejudice and discrimination through education and a philosophy of nonviolence—an approach that was very influential in the Civil Rights movement.

Third World Press
Box 730, 7524 S. Cottage Grove Ave.
Chicago, IL 60619
(312) 651-0700

Founded in 1967, the Third World Press publishes books by African Americans and others often ignored by mainstream publishers.

United Negro College Fund
500 E. 62nd St.
New York, NY 10021
(212) 326-1118

Founded in 1944, the UNCF raises funds for more than forty historically black colleges and universities and graduate and professional schools; UNCF scholarship programs have enabled many black students to obtain a college education.

12 Bibliography

Bearak, Barry, and David Lauter. "Affirmative Action: The Paradox of Equality." *The Los Angeles Times*, November 3 - November 5, 1991. This excellent three-part series focuses on affirmative action in the workplace, from the 1964 Civil Rights Act to the 1990's.

Branch, Taylor. *Parting the Waters: America in the King Years, 1954-63*. New York: Simon & Schuster, 1988. This Pulitzer Prize-winning study of the key decade of the Civil Rights movement is lengthy but compelling. Both the movement and King, its foremost leader, are illuminated.

Conover, Kirsten A. "Scholar Sees Culture at Risk." *The Christian Science Monitor*, November 5, 1991. Based on an interview with C. Eric Lincoln, a professor of religion and culture at Duke University, this brief article presents a pessimistic view of the situation of black youth today, particularly black males.

Dennis, Denise, *Black History for Beginners*. New York: Writers and Readers, 1984. This "documentary comic book" can be read in one sitting; good preparation for further study.

Edsall, Thomas Byrne, with Mary D. Edsall. *Chain Reaction: The Impact of Race, Rights, and Taxes on American Politics*. New York: W. W. Norton, 1991. This important book, which is critical of both conservatives and liberals, shows how racial issues have played a crucial — if often hidden — role in American politics since the 1960's.

Franklin, John Hope, and Alfred A. Moss, Jr. *From Slavery to Freedom: A History of Negro Americans*. 6th ed. New York:

McGraw-Hill, 1988. This classic history has been reworked so that it is as valuable today as it was when first published more than forty years ago.

Goddard, Connie. "Aiming for the Mainstream." *Publisher's Weekly* 239 (January 20, 1992): 28-34. One part of a special section on "Blacks & the Book World," this article reports that "African American publishers are doing more titles for a growing black readership"; includes a brief profile of Haki Madhubuti and his Third World Press.

Griffin, John Howard. *Black Like Me*. New York: Signet, 1960. Griffin, a white man who chose to experience pre-Civil Rights America with darkened skin, exposed the reality of life under segregation in this landmark book.

Hacker, Andrew. *Two Nations: Black and White, Separate, Hostile, Unequal*. New York: Charles Scribner's Sons, 1992. A wide-ranging study which attributes all the problems that beset the black community to white racism; includes abundant statistics.

Jaynes, Gerald D. and Robin M. Williams, eds. *A Common Destiny: Blacks and American Society*. Washington, D.C.: National Academy Press, 1989. An extensive report commissioned by the National Research council, this study analyzes the current status of blacks in American society. Includes beautiful illustrations in addition to many charts and tables.

Kozol, Jonathan. *Savage Inequalities: Children in America's Schools*. New York: Crown, 1991. A powerful report on the persistence of segregation and inequality in American elementary and secondary schools; emphasizes inequities in funding between inner-city districts and suburban districts.

Lederman, Douglas. "A Prize-Winning Playwright Seeks to Inspire." *The Chronicle of Higher Education*, November 27, 1991. A brief profile of Endesha Ida Mae Holland, author of the play *From the Mississippi Delta*.

Lewis, Neil A. "Black Judge's Success Story Begins in Cold Attic." *The New York Times*, July 19, 1991. The story of A.

Leon Higginbotham, Jr., whose experience with prejudice and discrimination prompted him to pursue a career in law.

Mead, Lawrence. *The New Politics of Poverty: The Nonworking Poor in America*. New York: Basic Books, 1992. Analyzes the increase in the number of nonworking poor people between the 1960's and the 1990's, focusing on long-term welfare mothers and nonworking single men, and considers various approaches to this problem.

Myers, Walter Dean. *Now Is Your Time! The African-American Struggle for Freedom*. New York: Harper Collins, 1991. Intended for younger readers, this excellent history extends from Africa in the eighteenth century to the Civil Rights movement in the 1960's. Includes fine illustrations. Myers is a black author of prizewinning fiction for young adults.

O'Hare, William P., et al. "African Americans in the 1990's." *Population Bulletin* 46 (July, 1991). This pamphlet provides a concise overview of the African American community at the beginning of the 1990's.

"Possibilities." *The New Yorker* 68 (February 24, 1992): 29-30. This unsigned piece from "The Talk of the Town" profiles the Raging Rooks, the Harlem junior high school chess team that became national champions, and Maurice Ashley, the young black chess professional who works with them.

Rainie, Harrison, et al. "Black and White in America." *U.S. News & World Report* 111 (July 22, 1991): 18-21. A brief but valuable assessment. Balances awareness of ongoing problems with recognition of genuine progress.

Schulhofer, Stephen J. "Access to Justice for the American Underclass." *The World & I* 6 (June, 1991): 462-475. Schulhofer shows how the poor are discriminated against in both the civil justice system and the criminal justice system.

Steele, Claude M. "Race and the Schooling of Black Americans." *The Atlantic* 269 (April, 1992): 68-78. Steele's analysis and recommendations draw on the work of black child psychiatrist James Comer; the article provides a good introduction to the Comer Method.

13 Media Materials

Boys N the Hood, 1991. Young black writer-director John Singleton goes beyond the headlines of gang violence in Los Angeles in this powerful portrait of inner-city life.

The Color Purple, 1985. Based on the best-selling novel by Alice Walker, this film shows black women ultimately triumphing over racism and sexism.

Do the Right Thing, 1989. Set in the predominantly black Brooklyn community of Bedford-Stuyvesant, this controversial Spike Lee film explores contemporary racial tensions.

Eyes on the Prize, 1986. In six hour-long segments this series chronicles the Civil Rights movement from World War II to the mid-1960's. Along with its sequel (see below), this PBS production is the best available introduction to contemporary African American history.

Eyes on the Prize II: America at the Racial Crossroads (1965-1985), 1987. The eight thirty-minute segments of this sequel document black Americans' ongoing struggle for equality.

Juice, 1992. Ernest Dickerson, Spike Lee's longtime cinematographer, made his debut as a director with this story of black teenage boys striving for "juice" or respect through increasingly dangerous, criminal, and self-destructive actions.

Jungle Fever, 1991. Centering on an interracial love affair, this Spike Lee film provokes examination of racial attitudes, both black and white.

Malcolm X, 1972. This 92-minute documentary, which was nominated for an Academy Award, includes footage from speeches by Malcolm and excerpts from interviews with him.

Martin Luther King: "I Have a Dream", 1990. This 28-minute video provides a brief overview of the Civil Rights movement and then presents King's "I Have a Dream" speech in its entirety.

Mississippi Burning, 1988. This film, set in the South during the Civil Rights era, has been faulted by some critics for underplaying the role of blacks in the struggle.

Straight Out of Brooklyn, 1991. The single-minded determination of young black director Matty Rich overcame all obstacles to get this story told: a true-to-life look at conditions for black youth today.

DISCRIMINATION

AFRICAN AMERICANS STRUGGLE FOR EQUALITY

INDEX